"Within these pages, you'll discover a curated collection of tried-and-true leadership tips, distilled from years of coaching executives and high-potential individuals. Read every word and become what you're meant to be – Indispensable!"
- **Dr. Marshall Goldsmith,** Thinkers50 #1 Executive Coach
and New York Times bestselling author of *The Earned Life*,
Triggers, and *What Got You Here Won't Get You There*

"*The Indispensable Leader's Handbook* is for anyone who wants to become an exceptional leader. Each tip is ready-made for quick consumption and immediate use. It's like having a super experienced leadership coach available on-demand!"
- **Dorie Clark,** Wall Street Journal bestselling author of
The Long Game and executive education faculty,
Columbia Business School

"This is not your typical business book; it's a comprehensive collection of advice on how to become an exceptional leader from one of today's top leadership voices."
- **Rhett Power,** CEO Accountability Inc. and
Forbes Contributor

"Jim's new leadership book grabbed me from word one! Of the many actionable insights he shares is the essential concept that we don't lead simply because of our title or position – we lead at every level, through our behavior, and that behavior needs to be honed, adjusted, and nurtured continually. Don't miss this book! It will inspire you to become the best leader and positive influencer you can be."
- **Kathy Caprino,** Career and Leadership Coach, Management Trainer,
Senior Forbes contributor, and author of *The Most Powerful You*

"James Kerr delivers more than just a book; this work is a coaching, guiding, and leadership program in print—an inspirational reference relevant to leaders at all levels."
- **Monte Pedersen,** Principal and Owner, The CDA Group, LLC

"Kerr knows that indispensable leaders inspire and develop others to become better than the best they ever knew. He delivers best practices for life; share his timeless principles with others and use them daily...I do."
- **Joe Polanin,** Captain, U.S. Navy (retired) and Founder,
The Alaka'i Leadership Group

"Direct and practical, the Indispensible's Leader's handbook sparkles with clarity and wisdom. If you've been looking for proven tips to up your leadership game, you've arrived."
- **Alain Hunkins,** CEO, Hunkins Leadership Group and Author,
Cracking the Leadership Code

The Indispensable Leader's Handbook

The culmination of 30 years of management consulting and leadership coaching, this collection of tried-and-true tips will make you a better leader when you work to make them yours.

Unlike other leadership coaching books, this is not a guide to help coaches improve their skills but to help leaders improve by folding coaching techniques into their leadership approach. It covers a wide variety of topics, from mindset to culture to change management, and each tip comes with a suggested action for executive, mid-level, and supervisory leaders, ensuring this book's value regardless of your current leadership role within your organization. Each of the 101 tips is also accompanied by its "why," Guru Guidance that outlines implications, and an Idea Crosswalk section that shows how each tip corresponds to other parts of the book to facilitate innovative thinking about how it can be best put to use.

Enabling good leaders to become exceptional ones by incorporating coaching skills into their leadership practices, this clear and practical reference guide will become a go-to resource for current and future business leaders, coaches, and mentors, as well as executive education providers.

James M. Kerr is a top-ranked leadership coach. In addition, Jim is a culture change expert, vision story developer, and business transformation authority. A 7x business author, his leadership podcast *The Indispensable Conversation* is highly regarded within leadership circles, which makes him a popular speaker at corporate events and conferences. Undeniably, it is Jim's strong dedication to demystifying complex leadership concepts that enables him to consistently develop and deliver cutting-edge solutions to his clients.

The Indispensable Leader's Handbook

101 Tips From a Top-Ranked Business Coach

James M. Kerr

Routledge
Taylor & Francis Group

NEW YORK AND LONDON

Designed cover image: © Getty Images

First published 2025
by Routledge
605 Third Avenue, New York, NY 10158

and by Routledge
4 Park Square, Milton Park, Abingdon, Oxon, OX14 4RN

Routledge is an imprint of the Taylor & Francis Group, an informa business

ISBN: 9781032728186 (hbk)
ISBN: 9781032710266 (pbk)
ISBN: 9781003422754 (ebk)

DOI: 10.4324/9781003422754

Typeset in Sabon
by Newgen Publishing UK

*For
My Mom
Elena*

Contents

About the Author

James M. Kerr is the #1 leadership coach worldwide according to Thinkers360, a watch group that tracks and rates over 6,000 professional coaches, consultants and academics around the globe.

In addition to leadership coaching, Jim is a culture change expert, vision story developer and business transformation specialist. A 7x business author, his leadership podcast *The Indispensable Conversation* is highly regarded within leadership circles. Jim is also a popular speaker at corporate events and conferences, speaking on leadership, culture and vision storytelling.

Industry independent, Jim's clients come from financial services, manufacturing, retail, and software, as well as federal, state, and local government and include such diverse organizations as The Home Depot, Bic, General Dynamics, Mitsui Sumitomo Insurance and the United States Marine Corps, to name a few.

It is his strong dedication to demystifying complex concepts that enables Jim to continue to develop and deliver cutting-edge solutions to his clients, while cultivating the fresh insights his coaching clientele require to become indispensable leaders.

Jim's other titles include:

- *Indispensable*
- *It's Good To Be King*
- *The Executive Checklist*
- *The Best Practices Enterprise*
- *Inside RAD*
- *The IRM Imperative*

Acknowledgments

Let me recognize some of the people who have made a difference to me while writing this book:

To Irene, Dylan, and Haley – thanks for giving meaning to my work;

To my mother, Elena and sister, Lisa – thanks for your unconditional support;

To Burgi and the rest of the extended family – thanks for keeping me grounded;

To all the folks in my LinkedIn tribe (while I can't name them all here), I do need to include the ones that "show up" for me most every day, including Dave Summers, Dino Carella, Joe Polanin, Timothy Hughes, Mahan, Tavakoli, Todd Cherches, Joe Iannone, Saliha Oukaci, Rob Longley, Ebony Travis Tichenor, Tony Martingnetti, Mandy Morris, Desiree Montejo, Mark Cumicek, Eric Stone, Bill Murphy, Sushma Verma, Tyler Schmoker, Marc Evans, Gareth Hosking, Damon Pistulka, David Marlow, John Chappelear, Rob Salafia, Claudia Wyatt, Peter Winick, Peter Gallagher, Céline Cloutier, Monte Pedersen and Marc Andersen – thanks for continuing to inspire me;

To my buddies, including Buyak, Blanchard, Steuernagel, Keough, Jones, Wardwell and Lee (full names withheld due to a few outstanding warrants for their arrest that may, or may not, exist) – thanks for the laughs that you provided along the way;

To my editors at Routledge, Meredith Norwich and Bethany Nelson – thanks for believing in the value of the book, and;

Thanks to all of my clients who helped me over the years to learn and to grow as I continue to hone my craft as a leadership coach and management consultant.

You are all indispensable leaders in my book.

A Word to the Reader

Above all, this is a leadership book.

The Indispensable Leader's Handbook contains some of my best thinking on the topic of leadership forged into tips that you can use to become the best leader that you can possibly be.

Like my other books, it is intended for one type of reader: a person who wants to be an indispensable leader – one that motivates and inspires the people they work with.

Whether you are a C-Suite executive looking to extend your leadership repertoire or a Gen Z staffer tackling your first leadership role, as long as you want to be an exceptional leader, this book is for you.

Anyone who regularly reads my *Psychology Today* or *Inc. Magazine* columns will recognize the style used to present this book's key concepts. Like most of the over 500 articles that I've published over the years, *The Indispensable Leader's Handbook* is written for quick consumption, fast reference and immediate use. I hope that you find this book achieves its purpose.

Lastly, *The Indispensable Leader's Handbook* is meant to be used every day. Its value comes through you putting the ideas into practice and shapeshifting them into your own. I know you have what it takes to bring these ideas to the next level!

With that, please read on, I promise it will prove to be indispensable.

Introduction

Welcome to *The Indispensable Leader's Handbook*

The aim of this book is to make you an indispensable leader – one so exceptional that you can't help but to inspire others to greatness. Indeed, I wrote the book for the betterment of you and the people whom you lead.

The Indispensable Leader's Handbook comes with decades of experience behind it. It is a culmination of the lessons that I've learned in over 30 years of management consulting and leadership coaching. In fact, I have been coaching leaders before it was "cool" to be a coach. My work has earned many accolades along the way. Most recently, Thinkers 360, a business advisory watch group that monitors and ranks the work of over 6,000 academics, coaches and consultants from around the globe, has ranked me the *#1 Leadership Coach* on the planet!

While the honor makes me blush, it's not one that I take lightly. For, it signifies substantial influence and impact within the professional community. Achieving the top spot on any of the watch group's lists means that one's insights are not only valuable but also resonate with a broad audience. However, the honor means very little if I fail to help YOU to become a better leader.

In an age where the online professional world is flooded with content, it's a challenge to find ideas that count. So, I've collected my favorite and most impactful tips. All are gleaned from the coaching work that I do with executives and their high-potential staffers. All are *tried and true*. To be sure, I am confident that each one will make you a better leader as you put it into practice.

Before we get to the first tip, though, let me share a bit about how the guide is organized.

DOI: 10.4324/9781003422754-1

About The Guide

This guide is structured into six (6) parts:

- Part I: *Leadership Mindset Tips*
- Part II: *Strategic Vision Tips*
- Part III: *Company Culture Tips*
- Part IV: *People and Talent Tips*
- Part V: *Trust and Empowerment Tips*
- Part VI: *Change Management Tips*

These six sections comprise *The Indispensable Leadership Taxonomy*. Each section contains subject matter that every leader must master to lead others, regardless of where that leader sits in an organization chart.

Which makes sense when you think about it: a leader must possess the right *mindset* to set a compelling *vision*, which helps to establish a winning *culture* that attracts the best *people* – ones who can be *trusted and empowered* to drive the *changes* needed for the organization to become indispensable in the hearts and minds of those whom they serve.

All 101 leadership tips are organized and presented using this taxonomy.

How The Tips Are Presented

Each tip is presented as a statement and is fortified by a brief comment outlining *why* the tip is relevant to you as a leader.

Guru Guidance is provided with each tip, too. Consider this as just some free advice from *yours truly* to consider as you begin to ponder the significance that each tip may have for you as a leader.

A short explanation of the tip comes next. It is intended to "round-out" your understanding of the tip's intent and meaning. These explanations are crisp and to the point for easy consumption.

This is followed by a *How to Put It Into Action* section. It offers three different suggestions on how to quickly put the tip into practice. Regardless of your current level within your organization (i.e., executive-level, mid-level, and supervisory-level), you get at least one idea for how to *jump start* your use of each tip.

To make the book ultra-useful as a quick reference source of leadership ideas, we've included an *Idea Crosswalk*, which delivers insights as to how each tip applies to and informs those found in the other parts of the book.

With that, it is my hope that you do use this guide as a reference source of leadership concepts and practices that will help to make you an indispensable leader, mentor and player-coach – one capable of achieving unprecedented results for your organization.

Now, let's take a look at the tips!

Part I

Leadership Mindset Tips

Indispensable leaders understand that their titles do not matter. Indeed, they understand that one's capacity to lead effectively is determined by competence, vision, and integrity rather than the level of authority granted by a title.

They bring the best out in the people whom they lead. They recognize the responsibility to set direction and inspire their people to bring their greatest effort to their work every day.

They recognize that decency counts. They understand that leaders can lead with empathy and a desire to do the right things.

The following tips are intended to enable leaders to develop the leadership mindset required to lead and direct others.

DOI: 10.4324/9781003422754-2

Leadership is a choice you must make each day

You don't lead because of title or position. You lead through behavior.

Guru Guidance

Reluctance on the part of some to assume a leadership role, even when they are the most qualified to take command often leads to organizational underperformance. To avoid this from happening, embrace opportunities to lead.

Leadership is not a static activity; leadership is an ongoing, dynamic, and challenging responsibility. The best leaders consistently set an example, provide direction, and maintain enthusiasm among their people.

Of course, choosing to lead means taking on the responsibility for making tough decisions and being accountable for their outcomes. So, making a daily commitment to staying intimately involved in the work and making adjustments to plans is required to give your people what they need to be most effective.

> *" . . . consistency in one's commitment to lead builds trust among team members."*

In fact, consistency in one's commitment to lead builds trust among team members. Leaders who consistently demonstrate their commitment to lead are more likely to earn the respect and allegiance of their team every day.

How to Put It into Action

For **Executive-Level Leaders** – Set the tone for what exceptional leadership looks like by choosing to actively lead your team each day.

For **Mid-Level Leaders** – Own the responsibility to lead your people by doing what is needed to set direction and manage the changes that transpire as they go about executing the mission of the organization.

DOI: 10.4324/9781003422754-3

For Supervisory-Level Leaders – Demonstrate that leadership is more than a title. Be the kind of leader that is present by actively participating in the work at hand.

Idea Crosswalk

- **Vision** – Include a discussion of the leadership mindset envisioned for the future of the company.
- **Company Culture** – Leaders shape the culture by persevering when things get tough.
- **People and Talent** – Your example shows your people what exceptional leadership looks like.
- **Trust and Empowerment** – Trust is built when leaders do what they say. Incorporate this practice into your leadership approach and inspire trust across the enterprise.
- **Change Management** – Leaders drive change by taking the helm. Be sure to lead your change efforts by being present and accessible.

Leadership is about them, not you!

Those leaders who mistakenly put their needs ahead of their teams find themselves leading demoralized and uninspired people.

Guru Guidance

Adopt a servant leadership mindset, where the primary goal is to serve and support the needs and development of team members. Make it clear that you are there to enable their success.

> " . . . the most effective leaders understand that their success is intricately linked to the success and well-being of their team . . . "

Leadership is fundamentally about serving the needs of the team or organization. After all, leaders exist to guide, support, and enable their team members to achieve their goals and the organization's goals. Indeed, the most effective leaders understand that their success is intricately linked to the success and well-being of their team, and they prioritize the needs and aspirations of their team members in their leadership approach.

By providing staffers with the resources, opportunities, and autonomy they need to succeed, the best leaders inspire and motivate others to bring their best effort to the job at hand.

Also, by setting an example of self-sacrifice and commitment to the team's mission, leaders motivate their teams to go above and beyond for the good of the organization.

Truly, it's tough to beat a thriving, motivated, and engaged team. For this reason, leaders who put the needs of their teams before their own establish the kind of trust within that team that gets the most of the people who comprise it.

DOI: 10.4324/9781003422754-4

How to Put It into Action

For Executive-Level Leaders – Put your team's interests first. Remain focused on your obligation to enable, support, and develop others within the enterprise. Back this focus up by investing in your people's growth and capabilities.

For Mid-Level Leaders – Make decisions that are in the best long-term interest of your team of leaders and the organization, even if they may not yield immediate personal benefits. Help your people understand why you chose to drive decision-making in this way so that they learn from your example.

For Supervisory-Level Leaders – Help individuals grow, acquire new skills, and reach their full potential, even if it means those team members may eventually move on to new opportunities.

Idea Crosswalk

- **Vision** – Your vision story should describe a workplace that recognizes and leverages the strengths of team members to achieve collective success.
- **Company Culture** – The public recognition and acknowledgement of the contributions and achievements of team members establishes a culture that gives credit where it is due.
- **People and Talent** – Leaders are best remembered within an organization for how they influenced and inspired others, not by their personal achievements.
- **Trust and Empowerment** – Approachable and accessible leaders inspire trust. Winning companies create an environment where individuals feel comfortable approaching their leaders with their ideas and concerns.
- **Change Management** – Your change management process should encourage collaboration and teamwork, emphasizing that the collective effort is more important than providing individual recognition for one's specific contribution.

Not every thought you have is a gem!

Recognizing this is the first step towards further developing your self-awareness and critical thinking.

Guru Guidance

Sometimes we become so enamored by our own ideas that we fail to see the flaws in our thinking. So, be sure to seek input and counsel from others on a regular basis.

As I often remind my clients, critical thinking means being critical of the quick deductions that we sometimes draw.

How?

Here are three tips to improve your ability to think past your initial inclinations:

> *" . . . recognize your own biases. We all have them . . . "*

- First, accept the fact that you're not always right. This is huge. Without it, you'll never see that you might need some critical thinking.
- Next, do your research. Get the data that you need to make your best, most-informed decision.
- Lastly, recognize your own biases. We all have them AND they can cloud our judgment.

If you do these things you will improve your decision-making outcomes, while overcoming the false belief that we know it all.

How to Put It into Action

For Executive-Level Leaders – Find a top executive coach that you can use as a sounding board. After all, we all need people to act as our sounding boards and to help expose us to our blind spots.

DOI: 10.4324/9781003422754-5

For Mid-Level Leaders – Bring a cohort leadership coaching program to your team of supervisory leaders. Not only will it improve their leadership skills, but the coach can help them identify ways to improve their self-awareness of how they are leading others.

For Supervisory-Level Leaders – Become a sounding board for your staffers. Work with each person on your team to assist in raising their consciousness of the biases that are playing a role in their day-to-day decision-making.

Idea Crosswalk

- **Vision** – Critical thinking and self-awareness are needed to craft a vision that others will buy into.
- **Company Culture** – Improved leader self-awareness will bring about a stronger, more accepting work setting.
- **People and Talent** – Your staffers will be more willing to offer opposing points of view if their leaders demonstrate a willingness to listen.
- **Trust and Empowerment** – Staffers will feel more appreciated when their ideas are validated by the people who lead them.
- **Change Management** – Change will be easier to institute when people have a chance to contribute their best thinking.

We ascribe meaning to everything we experience, so, choose wisely

You can reframe your thoughts to regulate your behavior.

Guru Guidance

Use this tip when you see that your people are getting lost in their own heads and dwelling on things that they cannot change.

> " . . . *it is up to each of us to decide how we will react to any situation . . .* "

It has been said that life is what you make it. When you consider that we all get to place meaning on the things that we see, think, and feel, you just might find that truer words have never been spoken.

Indeed, it is up to each of us to decide how we will react to every situation that we find ourselves in. We can absolutely lose our minds when things don't go our way. Likewise, we can choose to reframe our thoughts and recognize that overcoming adversity comes with the territory of leading others.

The choice is ours to make – lose our minds and the respect of our people; embrace the opportunity to demonstrate resilience and win the hearts and minds of those we lead.

So, choose your reactions wisely because your team is watching.

How to Put It into Action

For Executive-Level Leaders – Choose to maintain your composure when things go wrong and work with your colleagues to determine the best corrective action to pursue to right the ship.

For Mid-Level Leaders – Coach your team to shift their thinking when facing adversity. Work with them to see the opportunities that come with new challenges. Collaborate with them on the creation of solid solutions to address the matters at hand.

DOI: 10.4324/9781003422754-6

For Supervisory-Level Leaders – It's up to you to set the tone within your team. Do not focus on what went wrong or who to blame. Instead, define what must be done now to set things right.

Idea Crosswalk

- **Vision** – Character is fundamental to achieving the impossible. Weave this kind of ideal into your vision for the enterprise.
- **Company Culture** – Culture is a reflection of the way we think and behave. Recognize how one's thinking impacts the ways in which work is done within your organization.
- **People and Talent** – Encourage your team to regulate their reactions to adversity and you will contribute to creating a resilient work setting.
- **Trust and Empowerment** – An empowered workforce gets more done when it reframes failure as an opportunity to learn.
- **Change Management** – Don't let the unexpected bring out the worst in behavior during change efforts.

Expand your mind by seeking out different points of view

Diversity of thought always sparks levels of creativity and innovation that are not achieved otherwise.

Guru Guidance

Leaders often become insulated and, as a consequence, shut themselves off from receiving the kind of input that can lead to breakthrough thinking. Go out among your people and solicit their ideas for solving business problems.

Different viewpoints can lead to novel ideas and approaches that may not have arisen through isolated thinking. Intrinsically, diverse perspectives provide a broader and more comprehensive view of how to address business challenges. When leaders consider a range of viewpoints, they are more likely to make well-informed and better decisions.

> *" . . . seeking diverse points of view can help mitigate biases and blind spots."*

Further, seeking diverse points of view can help mitigate biases and blind spots. When leaders actively involve people with different perspectives and experiences, they are less likely to make decisions based on unconscious biases and stereotypes.

Of course, an inclusive environment where diverse voices are heard can boost employee engagement and morale, too. When employees see that their perspectives are valued, they are more likely to be motivated and committed to their work – which propels an organization towards greater achievement.

DOI: 10.4324/9781003422754-7

How to Put It into Action

For Executive-Level Leaders – Make our meetings a safe place for your top leaders to share their honest perspectives on business issues, without feeling the need to hold back out of a fear of reprisal.

For Mid-Level Leaders – Encourage your people to bring their best ideas forward, and respectively challenge one another when new ideas are surfaced with which they disagree.

For Supervisory-Level Leaders – Welcome different viewpoints. Be deliberate in developing the skills you need to turn conflicts into opportunities for growth and improvement among your team. When managed effectively, any conflicts that may arise can lead to better decisions and stronger team dynamics.

Idea Crosswalk

- **Vision** – Diversity of thought is an important characteristic to promote in your vision story.
- **Company Culture** – Diverse thinking makes for a culture that sees more options.
- **People and Talent** – Encourage the sharing of dissenting opinions among the staffers and watch how they work to become better at their jobs.
- **Trust and Empowerment** – Different perspectives and constructive debate enable trust to bloom.
- **Change Management** – Change management approaches must welcome dissenting points of view along the way – it is how an organization derives the best answers.

A foolish leader laughs at knowledge

Remember, no one knows all there is to know. Always seek learning opportunities.

Guru Guidance

One's ego can get in the way of learning. Remember to keep your ego in check because you always have more to learn.

Businesses and the social landscapes in which they operate are constantly evolving, driven by technological advancements, market shifts, and changing demographics. Leaders who continually learn are better equipped to adapt to these changes and steer their organizations in the right direction.

> *Leaders who acquire new knowledge and perspectives are more likely to generate fresh ideas and solutions . . . "*

Of course, learning fosters creativity and innovation. Leaders who acquire new knowledge and perspectives are more likely to generate fresh ideas and solutions, which is critical for staying competitive and addressing complex challenges.

Truly, leaders who prioritize learning send a clear message to their teams about the importance of self-improvement and growth. This serves to inspire employees to take ownership of their own development and invest in learning opportunities.

How to Put It into Action

For Executive-Level Leaders – Engage with other top leaders, whether through leadership retreats, conferences, or online communities. These interactions provide opportunities for networking and collaboration, which leads to developing broader perspectives and ideas for improvement.

DOI: 10.4324/9781003422754-8

For Mid-Level Leaders – Staying relevant to your business is a crucial measure of success. Promote continuous learning among your leaders so they stay up-to-date with the latest trends, best practices, and technologies within their areas of responsibility.

For Supervisory-Level Leaders – Learning is a lifelong journey that contributes to personal growth and development. Model a commitment to learning and set a positive example for your people – encouraging them to continuously learn and improve.

Idea Crosswalk

- **Vision** – Highlight a thirst to learn in your organization's vision for the future.
- **Company Culture** – A learning culture sets a high bar. It creates a place for continuous improvement.
- **People and Talent** – When leaders listen with intent to understand and to learn, they are modeling a behavior that helps their people to do the same.
- **Trust and Empowerment** – Don't become a leader that operates with the intent to implement a double standard – one that applies to your people and another that applies only to you.
- **Change Management** – You can't change what you don't understand. Be sure that your change initiatives begin by baselining the problem and characterizing the workplace with an honest assessment of the current state of affairs before determining change actions.

Only you can choose the leadership style needed for the situation

You need to develop several leadership styles to be truly effective.

Guru Guidance

Don't become a "one-trick pony" – using only one style of leadership, regardless of the situation that you find yourself in.

For today's leaders to be successful, they need to be adaptable, knowing when to use the "right" leadership style at any given moment. The fundamental styles were discussed by Paul Hersey and Ken Blanchard decades ago and still hold up today.[1] These include:

1. **Selling**. This style is used when leaders have to persuade team members who have the ability but who might be unwilling to take on a new or additional task. This tends to be used when charging a new team.

2. **Telling**. This style is used when leaders have to provide explicit direction and supervise work closely. Often used in managing a team right after they begin a new assignment.

> *"The fundamental styles were discussed by Paul Hersey and Ken Blanchard decades ago and still hold up today."*

3. **Coaching**. This style is used when leaders have to demonstrate the required work necessary and facilitate a team's learning process. This is used to help people to acquire the skills required to operate independently.

4. **Delegating**. This style is used when a leader feels confident in placing trust in a person or team to execute tasks according to their own judgment.

Of course, there are more sophisticated leadership styles that one can, and should, develop. However, most of those stem from one of these. Thus, it's essential to master the four above.

DOI: 10.4324/9781003422754-9

How to Put It into Action

For Executive-Level Leaders – Consider the capabilities, strengths, and weaknesses of your team members. Are they experienced and self-motivated, or do they require more guidance and support? Understand the dynamics of your team to determine what they need to operate at their highest capabilities.

For Mid-Level Leaders – Be flexible and adaptable. Recognize that the most effective leadership approach may change as the situation evolves. Be prepared to adjust your leadership style accordingly.

For Supervisory-Level Leaders – When a major initiative is completed, take time to reflect on the outcomes and the leadership approaches used. What worked well, and what could be improved for future situations? Learning from experience is essential for growth as a leader.

Idea Crosswalk

- **Vision** – An inspired organization comes from inspired leadership. Your vision should discuss the idea that leaders possess the skills and experiences needed to lead others through good times and bad.
- **Company Culture** – Leaders who know how best to lead will shape-shift the culture to one that is high in trust and integrity.
- **People and Talent** – Be sure that your team understands the "why," not just the "what." It is an essential part of knowing which leadership style is most appropriate to the current situation.
- **Trust and Empowerment** – Leaders who embrace this idea are more likely to remove barriers and create intra-organization connections to assist in getting things done within the enterprise.
- **Change Management** – The "right" style needed to successfully lead change shifts over time. So, leaders must develop a series of styles to be most effective.

Note

1 Hersey, P. and Blanchard, K.H. (1969). *Management of Organizational Behavior: Utilizing Human Resources*. Prentice Hall, New Jersey.

KISS and become easier to follow

Keep it simple, silly and they will beat a path to your door.

Guru Guidance

Don't "over-engineer" solutions to everyday leadership challenges – that only serves to confuse and frustrate your people.

> *"Business leaders have lost sight of the fact that simple is better..."*

Unfortunately, somewhere along the line in leadership circles, we have lost the meaning of KISS – Keep It Simple, Silly.

It seems that business leaders have lost sight of the fact that simple is better. Preferring, instead, to over-complicate much of what it takes to be a brilliant leader.

Consider some of the more popular leadership topics dominating current business thought pieces today:

- Emotional Intelligence
- Trust
- Empowerment
- Culture
- Engagement

All have inspired complicated and convoluted discussions by self-proclaimed leadership gurus attempting to rise above the "noise" and crowded space that is business thought leadership at the moment.

I prefer to keep things simple. I believe that if we treat people decently, they will follow us.

If you agree, let's take a step towards simplicity and position ourselves to be easier to follow.

DOI: 10.4324/9781003422754-10

How to Put It into Action

For Executive-Level Leaders – Know what's important. Keeping our focus on what's truly important to our organization's success helps us ignore the distractions that can lead to chaos and shambolic leadership.

For Mid-Level Leaders – When in doubt, trust your gut. Confidence is nothing more than remembering evidence of your own success. Of course, working with a coach can only help you draw wisdom from your experience. That said, when deciding on how to lead others, trust your record of accomplishment and seek to act graciously. Don't let self-doubt creep into your psyche and muddle your leadership method.

For Supervisory-Level Leaders – *Life Hacks* may be efficient, but they don't always promote quality leadership. Instead of looking for the easy way out, create a mindset that is willing to do whatever it takes to help your team win – even if that path requires more effort on your part than a shortcut that may leave destruction in its wake.

Idea Crosswalk

- **Vision** – Leadership that keeps things simple enables staffers to thrive. Make it a point of emphasis in your vision for the company.
- **Company Culture** – KISS will encourage staffers to find better ways to work and interact. A culture steeped in the value is likely to flourish over time.
- **People and Talent** – It's easier to get the job done when tasks are seen as simple. Help your talent thrive by seeking the simplest way to do the work of the enterprise.
- **Trust and Empowerment** – You can make KISS a value by practicing it. When you do, your organization's trust quotient will rise.
- **Change Management** – Create a workplace that can pivot on a dime by measuring the success of each change efforts on the basis of "doing simple better."

Leadership Tip 9

There comes a time to stop talking and start doing

To be most effective leaders need to know when to stop identifying every possible issue and take action.

Guru Guidance

While paradoxical, we wouldn't have so many problems if we didn't keep pointing them out! Joking aside, we can become our own worst enemy by deferring action for the sake of problem identification. Once possible scenarios are adequately determined, be the kind of leader that decidedly takes action and people will want to follow you.

Many leaders get so engrossed in problem identification that they forget that *true* leadership requires action.

Certainly, knowing the risks that surround a key decision is essential to minimizing risk. However, there comes a point of diminishing returns. Exceptional leaders keep this top-of-mind, and they know when to pull the trigger and take action.

In the end, we can become a roadblock to progress for the entire organization if we become too enamored in the process of identifying every possible issue that might derail our choice among options. Therefore, we must recognize that it's our responsibility to make the call.

> " . . . we can become a roadblock to progress for the entire organization if we become too enamored in the process of identifying every possible issue . . . "

How to Put It into Action

For Executive-Level Leaders – Recognize that avoiding a decision is in fact a decision. Stop overthinking every possibility and make the call.

For Mid-Level Leaders – Be aware that it is always shortsighted to kick a difficult decision down the road by pontificating about all of the possible

DOI: 10.4324/9781003422754-11

risks associated with it. Instead, when you have gathered enough situational awareness to determine a reasonable course of action, set it for all to follow!

For Supervisory-Level Leaders – It can be tempting to take the easy road and procrastinate in the name of minimizing risk. However, recognize that there is inherent risk in delaying necessary action. Work to develop your skill in knowing when it's time to stop talking about possible scenarios and take action.

Idea Crosswalk

- **Vision** – The best organizations have a vision of decisive leaders who properly manage risk.
- **Company Culture** – Too much emphasis on risk aversion can cripple organizational progress. Don't let this become part of your cultural dynamic.
- **People and Talent** – Staffers don't need to see their leaders struggle to take action. In fact, they respect those who gather information and make the call.
- **Trust and Empowerment** – As described, we promote trust and empowerment by encouraging people to practice a high degree of decision-making propriety.
- **Change Management** – Decisiveness is an essential key to keeping a change initiative on track.

Use current challenges to try new things and practice different approaches

Engaging your team to experiment by applying new ideas expands their capabilities.

Guru Guidance

Sometimes you must think out-of-the-box. Push yourself past the obvious and easy answers and seek elegance in problem-solving by applying a wider array of analysis techniques.

Complex problems often require multifaceted solutions. Employing a diverse set of analysis techniques helps leaders navigate the intricacies of complex issues, allowing for a more nuanced and adaptable problem-solving approach. In fact, it can help you to unearth better solutions to current challenges than the ones that would have otherwise been derived.

> *" . . . the work world has room for experimentation and learning."*

Keep in mind that the work world has room for experimentation and learning. It is a great place to try new ideas and test the concept of what is possible, as long as risks are recognized up front and deliberately managed.

By including others, you can explore unconventional solutions by incorporating varied perspectives, too. But, you have to be sure to create an open communications work environment that enables that to happen naturally. It just doesn't work when forced or contrived.

Indeed, applying a wider array of analysis techniques when problem-solving enables leaders to approach challenges with a more comprehensive and flexible mindset. This approach not only enhances the depth of understanding but also fosters innovation, collaboration, and adaptability among the people whom they lead.

DOI: 10.4324/9781003422754-12

How to Put It into Action

For Executive-Level Leaders – Be sure that each one of your problem-solving discussions begins with the end in mind. This kind of focus enables synergistic thinking to occur. Without a North Star to guide direction, a group can meander, and collaboration will suffer as participants become frustrated by the lack of focus.

For Mid-Level Leaders – Make collaboration the standard with your team by including every one of your direct reports in problem-solving activities.

For Supervisory-Level Leaders – Teach your team to draw on each other for insight and ideas by including a wide range of staff in your problem-solving huddles.

Idea Crosswalk

- **Vision** – Highlight advanced problem-solving practices in your vision for the enterprise.
- **Company Culture** – Don't we all want a culture that enables different kinds of thinking and problem-solving?
- **People and Talent** – Encourage synergistic thinking. This can have a positive impact on employee satisfaction and retention.
- **Trust and Empowerment** – Be patient and fair as your team learns – it is the best way to cultivate an empowered workforce.
- **Change Management** – The organization becomes more adept at handling change by embracing a variety of analysis techniques. Promote ideas to create change and foster innovation.

Leadership Tip 11

Remember, past success guarantees nothing!

Leaders must stay focused on today's mission and judge themselves on how well they are executing in the moment.

Guru Guidance

Yesterday's success does little to engage and inspire others today. Remember that active and engaged leadership is needed to help an organization to grow and flourish.

It's important not to rest on your laurels because complacency can lead to stagnation and missed opportunities for growth and improvement in the business.

Further, intense competition is a constant in the business world. New competitors, changes in market dynamics, and disruptive innovations will challenge even the most successful businesses. What worked in the past may not be sufficient to maintain a competitive edge in the future.

> *" . . . what worked in the past may not be effective in the future."*

Also, people follow their leaders. A leader's complacency sends a message to their team. If they think that you're OK with them being complacent, their growth and productivity will dip – and your business will go into a "competitive stall" as a result.

Remember, the world is constantly changing, and what worked in the past may not be effective in the future. Being adaptable and open to change is essential for long-term success.

How to Put It into Action

For Executive-Level Leaders – Push yourself past memorializing past successes. Innovation comes from pushing boundaries and exploring new

DOI: 10.4324/9781003422754-13

ideas. If you allow the business to become content with past achievements, it may miss opportunities to innovate and create greater value for its stakeholders.

For Mid-Level Leaders – Insist that your team of leaders learn and grow. Don't let them fall behind by getting too comfortable. Instead, use the thirst for more as the rationale for their regular leadership training and development.

For Supervisory-Level Leaders – Never be satisfied! Stay committed to pushing for more from your team and yourself. If you don't keep "pushing," enthusiasm for work will dwindle.

Idea Crosswalk

- **Vision** – Your vision must call for constant evolution. If allowed to stagnate, your competitors may surpass you, potentially leading to a decline in your market position.
- **Company Culture** – A company's culture is shaped by passionate and purposeful leadership. By fostering the thirst for more, you are laying the foundation for a winning culture.
- **People and Talent** – Push your team to stay current in their field of expertise, encouraging further growth.
- **Trust and Empowerment** – Display courage, optimism and ambition because that garners trust.
- **Change Management** – Inspiration is needed for change. Cultivating leaders who don't rest on their laurels ensures that change will be managed in a thoughtful and focused way.

Out of many, you are the one here, right now

Great leaders take full advantage of life's opportunities whenever and wherever they present themselves.

Guru Guidance

Carpe diem! It is essential that you seize the moment that you find yourself in, right now. If you don't, the opportunity to take the lead may forever pass you by.

I'm sure you know the meaning of the Latin term *carpe diem* – seize the day. But do you know the meaning of the Latin phrase e *pluribus unum*? It literally translates to "Out of many, one."

> *"You are a leader and people are relying on you to set the course and lead the charge."*

In fact, it is emblazoned across the Great Seal of the United States. The phrase refers to the emergence of a single nation out of the union of the original 13 colonies.

It also serves as a reminder for leaders that they have risen above to lead.

So, never doubt your reason for being here, right now.

You are the leader your people are relying on to set the course of action and lead them to success. So, seize the opportunity and lead the way you would want to be led. Show your team how right they are to follow you. Prove to yourself and your colleagues that you have what it takes to be an exceptional leader – now and into the future.

How to Put It into Action

For Executive-Level Leaders – Remind yourself on a regular basis that there are no guarantees in life. There may not be a tomorrow, so why not go for it today? You're a top leader for a reason, so lead!

For Mid-Level Leaders – Mid-level leaders get it from both sides – assignments from above and problems to fix from below. It is easy to become

DOI: 10.4324/9781003422754-14

so engrossed in the minutiae of the workday that you fail to see the opportunities to provide leadership where it is needed most. So, as soon as you get home from work, shut off your phone and don't turn it on until you return to work the next day. This will give you the mental break that you need to recognize the best ways for you to seize the opportunity to lead!

For Supervisory-Level Leaders – Confront the fears that are holding you back. One's fears get in the way of us living our professional lives to the fullest. Facing these fears and breaking through them will allow you to seize the opportunities before you.

Idea Crosswalk

- **Vision** – A vision story must be compelling. Fill it with notions of seizing opportunities that may seem unattainable at the moment.
- **Company Culture** – A healthy culture inspires people to dream big and take action.
- **People and Talent** – Staffers will respond well when encouraged to take advantage of the opportunities that work presents them.
- **Trust and Empowerment** – *Carpe diem* is always an empowering message. Use it to build trust within your organization.
- **Change Management** – By definition, change always presents an opportunity to snatch new opportunities for personal growth. Be sure the change processes that are in place enable your staffers to seize opportunities to take on new roles and responsibilities.

Clear your desk to clear your mind

Make time each week to examine how you led others and determine what worked and should be continued and what didn't go so well and should be improved.

Guru Guidance

Every leader needs to set aside a few moments at the end of each week to reflect on their leadership performance and to prepare for the challenges that they expect to confront in the week ahead. Make time to do this each week.

Allocating dedicated time each week to declutter your workspace of potential distractions is an essential practice. That itself can serve to center you. Use the opportunity, then and there, to engage in deliberate contemplation regarding your role as a leader.

> *"Assess your actions, acknowledging your strengths and areas where improvement is warranted . . . "*

Reflect upon the past week, particularly those instances where you exercised leadership. Assess your actions, acknowledging your strengths and areas where improvement is warranted for future leadership endeavors.

It is worth noting that this self-reflective process can illuminate blind spots, too. Identifying and understanding your blind spots not only enhances self-awareness but points to places where you can proactively address and enhance your leadership capabilities.

After all, personal change begins when we decide that the time has come to change.

How to Put It into Action

For **Executive-Level Leaders** – Continuous self-reflection is a hallmark of effective leadership. It allows leaders to adapt, grow, and remain

DOI: 10.4324/9781003422754-15

relevant in their roles over the long term, ensuring ongoing success for themselves and their organizations. Make time for it every day.

For **Mid-Level Leaders** – Self-reflection helps leaders adapt to changing circumstances. Encourage your people to regularly reevaluate their approaches and adjust their leadership styles as needed to meet evolving challenges in their areas of responsibility.

For **Supervisory-Level Leaders** – Reflect on past conflicts or challenges, and identify patterns and strategies for more effective conflict resolution the next time. Put them into practice and foster a better work environment, as you go along.

Idea Crosswalk

- **Vision** – A self-aware leader is more likely to have a clear understanding of their own values, strengths, and weaknesses, which they can weave into a compelling vision for the organization.
- **Company Culture** – When leaders understand their own values and behaviors, they can model authenticity, encouraging a culture where individuals feel empowered to be themselves.
- **People and Talent** – Self-aware leaders are better equipped to understand their own strengths and weaknesses, allowing them to assemble diverse and complementary teams.
- **Trust and Empowerment** – Transparency fosters trust within the organization. Team members are more likely to trust a leader who is self-aware, open about their limitations, and willing to learn and grow.
- **Change Management** – Leaders who regularly reflect on their leadership practices are more adaptable. Leadership adaptability helps to build a change-friendly work environment.

Work to accept what you can't control

Acceptance is a "superpower" that can help you to remain calm, cool and collected when things aren't going your way.

Guru Guidance

Help your people to move on when you see them struggling. Regret and rumination begets disappointment and saps motivation.

The key to practicing acceptance is recognizing what you can control and accepting what you can't control. Place energy and focus on what you control and you will begin reinvigorating your ability to choose patience over stress.

> *"whatever happens along the way won't be quite as frustrating . . ."*

After all, even if things don't work out the way that you wish, at least whatever happens along the way won't be quite as frustrating and anxiety-provoking to you because you've learned to accept what you can't change.

Additionally, your newfound ability to accept the things that are beyond your control will be a *strength* that enables you to become a more decent person and leader. People want to follow leaders who can accept circumstances that they don't control and who do not pretend to be in "charge" all the time.

How to Put It into Action

For Executive-Level Leaders – Foster a workplace culture that acknowledges challenges and encourages collaboration and support to overcome them. When teams work together, burdens become more manageable.

For Mid-Level Leaders – Help your team of leaders to see that they can't control everything within their area of responsibility. Show them that it is fine to accept what can't be changed, then help them to change those things that they can improve.

DOI: 10.4324/9781003422754-16

For **Supervisory-Level Leaders** – Don't resist what you can't change. Instead, remain diligent in improving what you can. Developing these skills will make you a better and more respected leader over time.

Idea Crosswalk

- **Vision** – Strong organizations learn to adapt to a changing world. Be sure your vision reflects this reality.
- **Company Culture** – A company culture that can adjust to situations that can't be controlled tends to be hardier in the face of adversity.
- **People and Talent** – Well-adjusted leaders, ones that can accept situations that they don't control, are more apt to develop resilient teams that possess the "right" mindset to overcome challenges.
- **Trust and Empowerment** – By acknowledging challenges and demonstrating a constructive approach to problem-solving, leaders can create a workplace where employees feel supported and trusted.
- **Change Management** – Leaders who practice acceptance are better prepared to manage crisis situations – minimizing the impact of uncontrollable events on the organization.

Forgive yourself when someone lets you down

This simply means you thought they wouldn't!

Guru Guidance

This tip applies in your personal life, too. It serves as a wonderful reminder that people in your life may not live up to your expectations in their thoughts and deeds. You must not punish yourself over this fact. Rather, forgive yourself for feeling badly about someone else's action and do what you can to control your own.

As an earlier tip suggested, high-performing people often dwell on things that are truly beyond their control. Just stop it!

We can never control what others do, or say, or think. With that, recognize that it is next to impossible for those in our workplace to always do what we want them to do. Colleagues will let us down. We can't castigate ourselves when they do.

> *"Colleagues will let us down. We can't castigate ourselves when they do."*

Instead, forgive yourself for misjudging others and remember that you can't change them, you can only change the way in which you react to how others behave.

Moreover, forgive the person that didn't live up to your expectations. This doesn't mean you are condoning the behavior, but the act of forgiving someone will release you from the burden of holding onto resentment.

Above all else, recognize that it is not a failing of yours when people let you down.

How to Put It into Action

For Executive-Level Leaders – Know that, despite your position or title, you are not the only person in the world who experiences "let downs."

DOI: 10.4324/9781003422754-17

Work to forgive yourself whenever you're feeling badly about mis-judging others.

For Mid-Level Leaders – Give yourself permission to make mistakes. Your judgments and expectations of the people whom you lead can be in error. When they let you down, remember that you're not infallible, and practice self-forgiveness, instead.

For Supervisory-Level Leaders – Think of these experiences, when a team member fails to do what you expected, as an opportunity to learn that you can't control everything. These experiences can hold the key to moving forward faster and more consistently in the future as you learn that you can only control yourself and your own behaviors and reactions.

Idea Crosswalk

- **Vision** – The vision story for your organization should have compassion for others as a theme.
- **Company Culture** – A culture that allows room for self-forgiveness enables everyone to perform at their best.
- **People and Talent** – You can expect people to make mistakes. Forgive them and yourself when they do.
- **Trust and Empowerment** – Open communication about disappointments can contribute to a culture of transparency and trust within the organization.
- **Change Management** – Planning and leading change is fraught with all kinds of opportunities for people to act in ways you wouldn't expect. So, learn to accept that your staffers may let you down. It will make your change effort easier to process.

Every great dream begins with a dreamer – a leader dreams big

Exceptional leaders cultivate their imaginations to inform their vision. It helps them to see what can be.

Guru Guidance

Leaders should prioritize self-reflection and introspection to better understand their own values and aspirations, which can serve to inform their vision for the organization. Encourage colleagues to incorporate this into their daily routines, too.

Have you properly cultivated your imagination to craft a vision that excites?

Remember, your vision needs to electrify you and the people whom you lead. If you can't get excited about the possibilities, how can you expect others to become energized by it?

> *" . . . your vision needs to electrify you and the people whom you lead."*

Of course, you will need some dedicated time and thought to do this envisioning justice. The goal should be to characterize a bold and exciting set of opportunities that you see your organization achieving.

But, keeping it realistic is essential. If your dream is too far out there and viewed as being widely impossible to achieve you will lose your staffers right out of the gate – most people will only get behind and support a vision that they see as being achievable.

With this guidance, give yourself the time needed to "dream big" so you have the fodder to craft a spellbinding vision that inspires you and your team to get after it!

How to Put It into Action

For Executive-Level Leaders – Gather a team of your best thinkers and begin to "brainstorm" the possibilities. Often, an outside facilitator

DOI: 10.4324/9781003422754-18

versed in vision story development can be instrumental to your success in this effort.

For Mid-Level Leaders – When it comes time to develop and implement the strategies needed to realize the stated vision, take the time needed to help your people "see" what you think will work for them and the organization. Give them your vision for how they should proceed and why.

For Supervisory-Level Leaders – Execution of the steps needed to achieve the strategic vision comes down to you to oversee. That being the case, be sure to provide your team with your "vision for action" that they can follow to do what must be done.

Idea Crosswalk

- **Vision** – A leader's bold dreams set an expansive and inspirational vision for the organization. When done right, it will motivate staffers to give their best effort to achieve it.
- **Company Culture** – When leaders articulate wide-ranging aspirations for the enterprise, they encourage the creation of a culture of innovation and risk-taking.
- **People and Talent** – Bold visions attract top talent-seeking opportunities for growth and for having an impact on the organizations that employ them.
- **Trust and Empowerment** – A leader's bold vision, when communicated effectively, inspires confidence and trust throughout the enterprise.
- **Change Management** – Your vision will provide the context for change. Be sure it's detailed enough to inspire commitment.

You must share your dream to make it come true!

People can't support what they don't understand. Share your dream and invite others to be part of it, too.

Guru Guidance

Clearly articulate why your dream for the organization is important and how it aligns with market trends, customer needs, and the competitive landscape. Providing context helps employees understand why they should buy-in and support the achievement of your vision.

Employees want to understand the broader purpose of their work. Sharing your dream for the organization will serve to align everyone with a common purpose. From there, it is up to each employee to ensure that their individual effort contributes to the collective success of the organization.

> *" . . . leaders demonstrate their openness to pivoting when better ideas are identified and pursued . . . "*

Indeed, sharing your vision helps create a sense of purpose, promoting enthusiasm and commitment to making the dream come true.

Further, engaged employees are more committed, innovative, and productive. As mentioned in an earlier tip, engaging employees emotionally creates a sense of ownership and pride in their work, leading to higher levels of engagement.

Leaders should share their dreams for the enterprise with staff members to inspire, align purpose, build trust, clarify direction, and engage employees. You would be remiss if you didn't share your vision for the organization with your staffers.

How to Put It into Action

For Executive-Level Leaders – Develop a strategic plan or roadmap that outlines the necessary actions, milestones, and resources required to

DOI: 10.4324/9781003422754-19

achieve your dream for the enterprise. This will serve as your guide on the path to realizing your vision.

For Mid-Level Leaders – Translate your top leader's dream into actionable steps that your team of leaders can execute from. Be sure to describe key milestones and outline the work that must be accomplished to determine success.

For Supervisory-Level Leaders – Consistently work with your team on the tasks and actions outlined in your leader's roadmap in order to contribute to the attainment of the vision.

Idea Crosswalk

- **Vision** – Leaders must define the strategic vision as precisely as possible in order to open up the organization to the realm of possibilities that exist for its realization.
- **Company Culture** – A culture characterized by a supportive network of colleagues who work together and are accountable to each other manifests when people share in pursuing a common vision.
- **People and Talent** – New knowledge, skills, and experiences that help staffers refine their approach to executing and overcoming obstacles is the bedrock of opening new avenues for the successful achievement of the vision.
- **Trust and Empowerment** – Failure is often a part of the journey toward any significant achievement. Trust is built when leaders view setbacks that occur along the way as valuable learning experiences that bring an organization closer to realizing its vision, instead of seeing them as insurmountable challenges that cannot be overcome.
- **Change Management** – Achieving a vision often requires persistence and determination, even when faced with challenges or setbacks. Both are necessary elements of any successful change initiative.

Part II

Strategic Vision Tips

Indispensable leaders envision what can be. A compelling vision of the future serves to inspire and motivate employees. When people understand the broader purpose and potential impact of their work, they are more likely to be engaged and committed to achieving their leader's strategic intent.

They tell stories to encourage engagement and understanding. From an early age, we are told stories to enable learning. The indispensable leader uses storytelling as a means to teach and rouse their teams to action.

Leaders help their people to see what's in it for them. People want something to believe in. But, to drive action, the best leaders understand that staffers need to see that achieving the vision will help them, too. Thus, every vision needs to show how each employee's personal success can be attained by making the vision a reality.

These tips help leaders to provide a compelling vision needed for unrestrained business success.

DOI: 10.4324/9781003422754-20

A leader envisions; a manager interprets

A leader needs to imagine what the business is to become and share that vision with their leadership team. Managers must understand that vision and drive their teams to do the specific work necessary to accomplish what has been expressed.

Guru Guidance

Strategic success comes when leaders provide an overarching vision and enable their managers to take responsibility for the practical implementation of it. This "division of labor" allows for a balanced and effective approach to execution.

> *"Articulate your vision and work to align the entire workforce on accomplishing it . . . "*

It is important to recognize this division of responsibilities between top leaders (who envision) and their team of leaders (who interpret and execute). Encouraging shared responsibilities contributes to the establishment of a dynamic synergy that propels the organization forward towards greater success.

But the vision must be vivid and compelling, and that's where you come in. Articulate your vision and work to align the entire workforce on accomplishing it – promoting a shared identity, and creating a sense of belonging among employees along the way.

Furthermore, next-level leaders play a critical role in managing the day-to-day execution of the work needed to attain top leadership's vision. After all, they are responsible for overseeing the implementation of projects and addressing operational challenges as the organization pursues the course of action required for achievement.

Ultimately, this combined effort of leaders and managers ensures that companies can navigate complexity, capitalize on opportunities, and overcome obstacles required to thrive within a dynamic marketplace.

DOI: 10.4324/9781003422754-21

How to Put It into Action

For Executive-Level Leaders – Be sure to communicate the vision using a variety of devices including in-person, recorded, visual depictions, and the written word to ensure your people understand it.

For Mid-Level Leaders – Work at determining the "how" of achieving the organization's goals. Communicate that interpretation to your team of leaders so they can bring that insight deeper into the organization.

For Supervisory-Level Leaders – Place the bulk of your effort on optimizing the allocation and management of your resources, ensuring that day-to-day operations align with the larger strategy.

Idea Crosswalk

- **Leadership Mindset** – Leaders must focus on defining the "what" and "why" of their organization's mission, communicating that in ways that their employees can comprehend and take action to accomplish.
- **Company Culture** – Leaders can reshape company culture by demonstrating their commitment to the vision and values through their own actions and decisions.
- **People and Talent** – Cascading communication, top-to-bottom as described gives staff what they need to choose to engage.
- **Trust and Empowerment** – Trust is built when there is an alignment of leadership messaging and behavior that reinforces the organization's stated purpose and mission.
- **Change Management** – By explaining why the vision is important and how it aligns with the organization's mission and values, team members better understand the bigger picture and the importance of their change efforts.

An organization can only become what its leaders imagine it to be

Leaders are the architects of their organization, shaping its values, goals, and strategies. Without a clear and inspiring vision, an organization can drift aimlessly, lacking purpose and identity.

Guru Guidance

Infuse your vision with a sense of passion and commitment, emphasizing the positive impact the organization can make on its stakeholders and the world. It makes your vision come alive!

A leader's vision is the driving force behind an organization's direction and success. In fact, a leader's vision serves as a source of motivation and inspiration for employees. When leaders imagine a compelling future for the organization and communicate it effectively, they align their workforce to achieve a common set of goals. This alignment empowers employees to work together synergistically, leveraging their collective skills and efforts to bring their "common vision" to fruition.

Moreover, leaders play a crucial role in fostering innovation and adaptation within an organization. Their stated vision serves as the North Star, allowing the organization to more effectively navigate through the ever-changing business landscape.

> *"Their stated vision serves as the North Star, allowing the organization to more effectively navigate . . ."*

What's more, by envisioning a dynamic and resilient organization, leaders empower their teams to embrace change, seize opportunities, and evolve in response to new circumstances.

In essence, an organization can only become what its leaders imagine because leaders are the visionaries who shape a firm's identity, inspire its members, and steer it toward a worthwhile future.

DOI: 10.4324/9781003422754-22

How to Put It into Action

For Executive-Level Leaders – Challenge your team of leaders to help with identifying and establishing ambitious and aspirational goals that can serve to underpin your vision.

For Mid-Level Leaders – Your job is to translate the vision into action. As you do, be sure to acknowledge and celebrate your managers who take calculated risks and step outside their comfort zones to drive employees towards the achievement of the stated vision.

For Supervisory-Level Leaders – Take action to make the vision a reality. Be sure to encourage your team members to contribute their ideas and opinions on how to best get the work accomplished without fear of criticism.

Idea Crosswalk

- **Leadership Mindset** – Top leaders must make the time to envision the future of their organizations and articulate that vision in ways that engage and inspire.
- **Company Culture** – Company culture is shaped by the vision of its leadership team. So, of course, leaders must ensure that it's understood so to drive cultural change.
- **People and Talent** – Middle managers and supervisors should be recognizing their role in institutionalizing the vision by translating it into action and overseeing the work necessary to achieve it.
- **Trust and Empowerment** – Placing emphasis on the positive impact that the achievement of the vision will make for the "greater good" can arouse the staff's commitment needed to realize it.
- **Change Management** – All organizational change must align with the vision. If a proposed change doesn't contribute to the achievement of the vision, it should not be pursued.

Take the long view

Lasting success is not achieved by winning a few occasional sprints; it comes by maintaining pace in a world-class marathon.

Guru Guidance

It's common for leaders to become caught up in attaining short-term goals. This kind of thinking can lead to organizational failure in the marketplace. Be sure to keep an eye on the bigger picture and do what is necessary to position your business for enduring success.

> *"If we allow ourselves to be so laser-focused on today, we will surely lose sight of the larger strategic intent ... "*

Certainly, leaders play a critical role in pushing staffers to deliver in the short term. However, this should not be our sole purpose in leading others. If we allow ourselves to be so laser-focused on today, we will surely lose sight of the larger strategic intent that must be attained to ensure the lasting success of the enterprise.

By adopting a bigger-picture mindset, we help to instill the same attitude in our staffers. This creates a ripple effect throughout the organization, and it promotes a sense of common purpose and focus on executing the mission. Teamwork, resilience, and adaptability improve as a result, too.

Indeed, it's our job to think bigger and help our people to maintain a longer-term perspective, too. This kind of mindset is important to cultivate because it encourages leaders to consider long-term goals, overarching objectives, and the holistic well-being of the organization as they go about doing the daily work of the enterprise.

DOI: 10.4324/9781003422754-23

How to Put It into Action

For Executive-Level Leaders – Invest in building a culture that promotes long-term thinking, and reward your top leaders for their contribution to achieving the strategic objectives necessary to flourish in the future.

For Mid-Level Leaders – Give your people the time that they need to consider the long-term vision for the enterprise. Don't fall into the trap of driving them to achieve short-term goals at the expense of never realizing lasting strategic objectives.

For Supervisory-Level Leaders – While hitting quarterly numbers is essential, recognize that the long-term, bigger picture must remain in focus. Make sure your performance metrics are aligned with your team's overarching responsibilities.

Idea Crosswalk

- **Leadership Mindset** – By definition, vision attainment is a long-term endeavor. Seldom are they achieved overnight.
- **Company Culture** – It is essential to build a culture that works today and positions an organization for long-term achievement tomorrow.
- **People and Talent** – Bringing perspective to both short-term and long-term goals provides staffers with the awareness needed to maintain proper focus on both.
- **Trust and Empowerment** – Offering the long view is part of providing your people with the "why" that they need to trust your leadership.
- **Change Management** – Changes are always accompanied by a period of lower productivity for teams until everyone is able to adjust. So, incorporate this fact into your planning of change initiatives.

Embrace "Outside-In" to win!

We gain needed perspective when we see how our business operates through an outsider's lens.

Guru Guidance

Conduct role-playing exercises to simulate the perspectives of different stakeholders. Encourage your people to step into the shoes of a customer, investor, or trading partner and assess how the organization's actions and decisions might be perceived from that perspective.

Take a moment and try to see your business through the eyes of its customers. Do you like what you see? Are we operating with the best interests in mind? Do we treat them with respect and recognize that they are the ones that determine our success?

The answer to these questions better be a resounding: "*Yes!*"

To ensure this, place an emphasis on developing your team's knowledge and skills. Make sure they have what is necessary to delight your customers.

> "*Take a moment and try to see your business through the eyes of its customers.*"

Further, share with them a perspective on the greater purpose behind their work and how it influences the customer and the internal workings of the company. This sense of purpose can inspire higher levels of performance.

Indeed, your people should be taught to question whether their decisions and actions will ultimately benefit the customer and they should be encouraged to make prompt changes in processes, policies, and behaviors that do not help your customer achieve their goals.

DOI: 10.4324/9781003422754-24

How to Put It into Action

For Executive-Level Leaders – Invest in market research, surveys, and customer feedback to gain a deep understanding of your customers' needs, pain points, and expectations.

For Mid-Level Leaders – Commit to instilling a customer-centric mindset throughout the organization. Make it clear to your team that satisfying customers is everyone's responsibility.

For Supervisory-Level Leaders – Work with your front-line staff to map out the entire customer journey to identify pain points and opportunities for improvement. Streamline processes to make it easier for customers to do business with you.

Idea Crosswalk

- **Leadership Mindset** – You can't compromise your ideals by pursuing profit over service delivery. If you do, customers will walk.
- **Company Culture** – The culture must have "customer-first" values baked in.
- **People and Talent** – Your people should operate with the "impact on the customer" in mind.
- **Trust and Empowerment** – Empower your people to do whatever it takes to deliver on promises made to the customer.
- **Change Management** – Make changes that will provide value to the customer and that you will continue to motivate their commitment to doing business with your organization.

Being indispensable is the ultimate customer experience metric

It means that your business is one that customers can't live without.

Guru Guidance

We don't define the customer experience, customers do! Take the steps needed to ensure that you're delivering an experience that will keep them coming back for more – and not the kind of experience that will send them on a mission to find a better provider.

> "If you can't give them what they want, in the way that they want it, someone else will."

Please believe that regardless of what your company does or how it does it, there's another firm right behind you ready to take your spot. Moreover, your competition is not just local businesses. It's global. You already know why this is true; the business world is a whole lot smaller today than it was even just ten years ago. So, competition exists all over the planet and you have to respect that.

Indeed, your customers have choices. If you can't give them what they want, in the way that they want it, someone else will. It's just a point-and-click away. So, you better figure out quickly just how to become indispensable or you just might be replaced.

It's our job as leaders to deliver the kind of customer experience that keeps them coming back for more. What's more, it's our job to ensure that our businesses are the ones that customers prefer over any others in our space.

So, use indispensability as the ultimate customer experience metric to ensure you're doing all that you can to be "of choice" in the markets that you serve.

DOI: 10.4324/9781003422754-25

How to Put It into Action

For Executive-Level Leaders – Regularly poll your team of top leaders if they believe the enterprise is indispensable to your customers. If not, ask them what needs to be done to make that so. Fold those answers into your strategic planning.

For Mid-Level Leaders – Align your functional responsibilities with the vision of becoming the business that your customers can't live without. By designing work around the customer you will begin to naturally identify ways to improve your business operations.

For Supervisory-Level Leaders – Identify and institute metrics within your area of responsibility that measure your customer's preference for doing business with you over any other option available to them in the marketplace.

Idea Crosswalk

- **Leadership Mindset** – The customer experience determines your long-term business results.
- **Company Culture** – The customer experience must remain top-of-mind so that your staffers can help you reshape the workplace culture accordingly.
- **People and Talent** – See the organization through the eyes of whom you serve. When you do, you will see the best way to develop a team of people that can deliver on customer expectations.
- **Trust and Empowerment** – Doing right by the customer is the ultimate in employee empowerment.
- **Change Management** – When deciding among change options, place your customer's needs ahead of your own and use those to dictate the direction for, and goals of, the change effort.

Give them something to rally around!

Goals and objectives are rarely motivation enough to get the best out of your people. They need something that strikes an emotional chord that they can get behind and fight for.

Guru Guidance

Researching and analyzing competitors' products, pricing strategies, marketing efforts, customer reviews, and market positioning can help illustrate how fierce the fight for market superiority has become. Use these insights to establish your competition as the enemy that must be defeated.

Too many organizations have work environments that accept political in-fighting. This can sabotage any hope of achieving the strategic vision.

Thus, it behooves us to remember that people are more likely to work together when they understand that their organization is under constant attack by the competition.

> *" . . . people are more likely to work together when they understand that their organization is under constant attack by the competition."*

Indeed, we can elicit stronger staffer commitment to the achievement of the strategic vision by positioning competitors as adversaries.

With that, the vision must be shared widely and promoted regularly so that it remains in the forefront of your people's collective minds as they go about their work each day. If not, the *common cause* that serves to engage and inspire them to do their best may fade.

Of course, too much emphasis on threats can lead to stress and burnout too. So, work to strike a balance on the common threat messaging. After all, we can't ever neglect the fact that it's on us to create an environment that encourages teamwork and achievement without fostering a culture of fear.

DOI: 10.4324/9781003422754-26

How to Put It into Action

For Executive-Level Leaders – Inspire your people by giving them a "rallying cry" – someone to fight, or something to fight for, that exists outside of the four walls of the organization.

For Mid-Level Leaders – Highlight key customers' needs and encourage them to work with you to make the changes needed to deliver on those expectations – occasionally reminding them that there are competitors out there that would love to serve these customers.

For Supervisory-Level Leaders – From time to time, remind your team why you're in business. Help them understand the importance of not taking your customers for granted because those customers always have other options to meet their needs.

Idea Crosswalk

- **Leadership Mindset** – Display courage, optimism, and drive as you present your vision as a rallying cry.
- **Company Culture** – The cultural impact on pursuing and achieving a vision that leads to victory in the marketplace should be part of the story.
- **People and Talent** – Leadership support, resources, and tools that enable people to step up and deliver must be part of the talent development strategy.
- **Trust and Empowerment** – We build trust when we empower our staffers to do what they must to achieve the vision.
- **Change Management** – Part of ascribing the "why" of any change initiative should include an explanation of the necessity of making the change in order to better compete and win.

Make vision work a team-building activity

Engage your entire organization in the process of shaping the vision and gain unfettered commitment to the organization's new strategic direction.

Guru Guidance

Think of the organization being comprised of leaders, managers, and staff. Be sure to involve each group in the development of the vision story. For example, top leaders can be interviewed, managers can participate in group workshops and staff can be polled to solicit input.

> *"Invite them to be part of creating that future alongside you."*

How do you craft a vision story that really gets people excited and ready to take action? Invite them to be part of creating that future alongside you.

After all, it's not just about telling your staffers what the future will look like. In fact, no vision story can identify every single detail about the future organization, anyway. What's really important is to help your people to understand that it is their choices and behaviors that will shape the future, too.

So, why not give them a say? Why not actively involve them in the process of determining the vision for the enterprise?

Everyone wins when you get your team onboard to help drive the company forward. Truly, your staffers gain the opportunity to grow and develop as individuals, as the business thrives.

Encourage all of your staff members to take part in the vision development process. The process will expand their thinking and help them to gain fresh perspectives along the way. It's a journey worth taking together with your team!

DOI: 10.4324/9781003422754-27

How to Put It into Action

For Executive-Level Leaders – Make the strategic plan the centerpiece of the vision work. Get your team of top leaders to "own" their piece of it and then establish the level of cooperation required for all of them to succeed.

For Mid-Level Leaders – Generate excitement among your team of operational leaders by selling them on the fantastic opportunity they gain through their involvement. Highlight how their work on the vision enables them to shape the enterprise for the future.

For Supervisory-Level Leaders – Review the vision with your team and challenge them to take action and work together on improving the areas of it that mean the most to them. This way, you're not only engaging them in pursuing the vision, but you're also making their voices and passions an integral part of the journey.

Idea Crosswalk

- **Leadership Mindset** – The notion reinforces the idea that leadership is a "team sport!"
- **Company Culture** – Employee involvement in vision work helps to shape-shift the culture.
- **People and Talent** – Engaging staffers in vision work provides an opportunity to develop talent through exposure to work that they may not ordinarily be part of.
- **Trust and Empowerment** – It helps to ensure the team understands the "why," not just the "what," which enhances trust throughout the organization.
- **Change Management** – The conversations that transpire through the process will assist in gaining early buy-in to future change efforts.

Leadership Tip 25

A vision is best delivered as a story that people can relate to

Vision stories are powerful and effective ways to communicate strategic intent.

Guru Guidance

Leaders should work to transcend language and cultural barriers in their vision stories because that will make it easier for them to better communicate their strategic ideas to all stakeholders regardless of background and experience.

Stories have the power to inspire and motivate. When a strategic vision is presented as a story, it can create an emotional connection, instill a sense of purpose, and inspire individuals to work toward realizing common goals.

> *"... vision stories require a clear and focused narrative to accomplish this connection."*

When people understand the "why" behind the vision and see themselves as being successful within the story, they are more likely to align their actions and decisions with the company's strategic goals.

To be sure, vision stories require a clear and focused narrative to accomplish this connection. When well-structured, the narrative will help employees and stakeholders understand the vision far better than any list of bullet points or technical jargon can ever accomplish.

In fact, an exceptional vision story enables a senior leadership team to distill complex ideas into a coherent and understandable message, which brings about better decision-making and execution among the rank and file.

How to Put It into Action

For Executive-Level Leaders – Make vision story development a team effort. Engage your top leaders in developing story elements. You can

DOI: 10.4324/9781003422754-28

even ask them to craft sections of the story that pertain to their areas of responsibility.

For Mid-Level Leaders – Solicit your team of supervisors for ideas that they have to make the story more compelling to their teams, then ask them to bring the story down to their people using story elements that tap into those emotions, which can create a deeper connection to the vision.

For Supervisory-Level Leaders – People are more likely to support and advocate for a vision that resonates with their ambitions. Be sure to present key vision story elements to your team in ways that align with their personal goals and aspirations.

Idea Crosswalk

- **Leadership Mindset** – We learn by hearing stories that inform and inspire. As such, storytelling is a skill every exceptional leader must develop.
- **Company Culture** – Stories shape and reinforce company culture. By presenting the strategic vision as a story, leaders can embed the company's values, mission, and desired behaviors into the narrative, helping to create a culture that supports the vision.
- **People and Talent** – When a strategic vision is presented as a compelling narrative, it's more likely to stick in people's minds, making it easier for them to recall and share with others.
- **Trust and Empowerment** – Vision stories can be used to describe an enabled, confident, and empowered workforce positioned for success.
- **Change Management** – People remember stories much better than facts and figures. As such, a vision story can serve as the backdrop of any enterprise-level change initiative.

Your vision must describe what it means to better your best

Use the vision story to raise the bar for performance and results!

Guru Guidance

Be sure to work at establishing a mindset of never settling for the status quo and always striving for excellence. When you do, your vision storytelling will begin to naturally inspire stakeholders to adopt that mindset, too.

> *"It demonstrates a commitment to pushing boundaries and taking calculated risks . . . "*

In a competitive business environment, striving to be better than your best can give your organization a competitive edge. It means you are not just keeping up with competitors but surpassing them, which leads to market leadership. It also demonstrates a commitment to pushing boundaries and taking calculated risks, which can inspire confidence and trust in the leader's ability to guide the organization.

Additionally, a vision that calls for bettering your best effort fosters a culture of continuous innovation. This, in turn, encourages employees to think creatively and seek new solutions to achieve unprecedented levels of success – both are needed to "win" in the hyper-competitive business world today.

Undoubtedly, a vision story that calls for an organization to be better than it was before is a powerful motivator, attracting talent, driving innovation, and positioning the enterprise for sustained success – even in the face of constant challenges from competitors.

How to Put It into Action

For Executive-Level Leaders – Use the idea of "being better than before" to motivate and inspire higher performance among your team of leaders. Be sure that they understand that the aim is to surpass the

DOI: 10.4324/9781003422754-29

organization's current achievements and challenge themselves to motivate their employees.

For Mid-Level Leaders – Your next-level managers need to develop the ability to overcome obstacles. Amplify this message of working to always *bettering your best* by pointing out that the organization needs this to achieve something exceptional.

For Supervisory-Level Leaders – Work to help your people believe that they are working toward something extraordinary. It creates a sense of purpose and excitement.

Idea Crosswalk

- **Leadership Mindset** – Exceptional leaders know that it's not just about short-term gains but about building a legacy of excellence.
- **Company Culture** – The use of this tip can drive innovation and progress within an organization's culture.
- **People and Talent** – When people are inspired to reach beyond what they have already accomplished, they are more likely to push their limits and achieve remarkable results.
- **Trust and Empowerment** – Greater empowerment of staffers is required to enable an organization to consistently strive to be better than it was yesterday.
- **Change Management** – This idea encourages employees to think creatively and seek new solutions to achieve unprecedented levels of success – which is essential to making change happen.

You can leave the numbers out of the story

It leaves room for the people in the organization to be creative in their pursuit of the vision.

Guru Guidance

People are not motivated by numbers! Instead, focus on the narrative to make your story "pop."

Excessive use of numbers in a story can lead to information overload, causing an audience to disengage.

Since we were children, we have been inspired by captivating stories of a better future. Leaving numbers out of your vision story makes it more relatable and emotionally engaging, encouraging buy-in from team members and stakeholders, alike.

> *"Leaving numbers out of your vision story makes it more relatable and emotionally engaging . . . "*

Also, a vision that is not cluttered with specific financial targets fosters creativity and innovation. In this way, your people are free to come up with more ingenious solutions and strategies that may surpass any numbers one might want to add to the vision story, anyway.

Indeed, by sidestepping the addition of specific numbers, leaders help to establish a longer-term perspective for their people. Rather than placing the focus on hitting quarterly or annual goals, promote enduring values and work principles. These are the fodder needed to inspire ongoing change and a thirst for excellence.

After all, there will be plenty of opportunities for leaders to communicate clear, measurable financial objectives and performance metrics in the strategic plans and operational forecasting that naturally follows strategic vision work.

DOI: 10.4324/9781003422754-30

How to Put It into Action

For Executive-Level Leaders – Use metaphors, stories, and anecdotes when sharing your vision for the enterprise. This creates an emotional connection with the vision for your stakeholders.

For Mid-Level Leaders – Inspire your team of leaders to work towards achieving shared results by focusing on the "so what" rather than the "how much."

For Supervisory-Level Leaders – When discussing the vision with your team, talk about becoming the best, achieving excellence, making a difference, and transforming the organization without attaching numerical values to these concepts.

Idea Crosswalk

- **Leadership Mindset** – When setting direction, leaders should emphasize the impact their organization aims to make, instead of the profits it seeks to earn.
- **Company Culture** – It is heartening to see employees come together, pooling their resources and leveraging their collective strengths to achieve a strategic outcome – chasing numbers just doesn't inspire that kind of collaboration.
- **People and Talent** – Numbers are tough to get emotionally connected to. When the vision is broad and inclusive, team members are more likely to take ownership of the vision.
- **Trust and Empowerment** – Trust builds with a consistent vision story as a framework. By leaving the numbers out, leaders can adjust strategies and tactics without having to justify deviations from predefined financial targets.
- **Change Management** – When the focus of a change effort is on a problem to solve or a need to be met, project team members are free to be more creative in their approach to the work at hand.

Remember that we are all just the sidekicks in our people's hero journeys

The hero's journey is not limited to mythological or fictional narratives; it is a reflection of the human experience. Why not leverage this when developing an organization's vision story?

Guru Guidance

Leaders who recognize that each person in an organization is in the process of undertaking their own hero's journeys while at work (i.e., facing challenges, growing, and achieving transformation), can use it to craft vision stories that make their people heroes.

Joseph Campbell was a renowned American mythologist and writer who extensively studied and wrote about the concept of the hero's journey.[1] His teachings have had a profound impact on literature, film, psychology, and the study of mythology. They continue to influence storytellers to this day.

> *" . . . the hero undergoes a profound transformation, gaining new insights and abilities."*

In the hero's journey, the protagonist receives a call to adventure, often in the form of a challenge or a quest. These challenges test their commitment and determination for success. By overcoming the challenges, the hero undergoes a profound transformation, gaining new insights and abilities. This personal evolution signifies the hero's growth and acceptance of new responsibilities.

Leaders should seek to weave this kind of content into their vision stories to firmly engage and stir their people to take up the pursuit of the vision for the organization, emphasizing how leaders are merely "sidekicks" who advise and assist personnel as they overcome the challenges that must be confronted to enjoy success.

DOI: 10.4324/9781003422754-31

How to Put It into Action

For Executive-Level Leaders – Rather than seeking personal glory, accept the role of sidekick emphasizing how you are contributing to the collective success of each member of your top leadership team.

For Mid-Level Leaders – By adopting a sidekick mindset, you will recognize that you don't always need to be the hero. This can lead to a healthier and more balanced approach to life and enable your team to bask in the glory of success.

For Supervisory-Level Leaders – Work to provide support, encouragement, and assistance to your people, making them the heroes who are achieving great things for the organization.

Idea Crosswalk

- **Leadership Mindset** – Acknowledging our role as sidekicks fosters humility and reminds us that we are not always the central character in every story.
- **Company Culture** – This approach to storytelling fosters mutual respect and understanding within an organization, leading to a more meaningful work setting for staffers.
- **People and Talent** – Many people find fulfillment in serving others and helping them achieve their goals. Leaders embracing the sidekick role can provide a sense of purpose and satisfaction for everyone in the company.
- **Trust and Empowerment** – The idea of leaders contributing to the betterment of their people is highly motivating and builds greater trust among an organization's workforce.
- **Change Management** – Adopting this idea emphasizes the value of teamwork, support, and collaboration in achieving the strategic goals of the enterprise – all critical for leading successful change management activities.

Note

1 Wikipedia, Joseph Campbell Page: https://en.wikipedia.org/wiki/Joseph_Campbell.

Let the vision drive your decisions

By embedding the strategic vision into your decision-making processes, you ensure that every choice made, at all levels of the organization, aligns with the organization's long-term objectives.

Guru Guidance

It is critical that decisions be made to further the organization's progress towards the achievement of its vision. As such, leaders must develop a formal decision-making framework that screens for strategic alignment.

> "Strategic options should be assessed on their degree of alignment with the vision."

It is top leadership's responsibility to ensure that their vision is used as a guiding light for decision-making. Strategic options should be assessed on their degree of alignment with the vision. Further, short-term and long-term consequences of each option should be considered so to inform final decision-making.

That said, it is important to regularly review and reflect on the outcome of key decisions – analyzing whether each decision moved the organization closer to, or further from, strategic vision fulfillment. Doing this reinforces the institutionalization of a decision-making framework anchored on vision achievement.

Additionally, the practice reduces something, I call "shiny object syndrome" – the squandering of assets in the pursuit of ideas and opportunities that are inconsistent with an organization's strategic ambitions.

It is never wise to pursue notions that veer an enterprise off its stated vision for the future.

How to Put It into Action

For Executive-Level Leaders – Develop a strategic framework or model that outlines the key elements of the vision and the criteria for evaluating

DOI: 10.4324/9781003422754-32

strategic options. This framework should include factors such as market trends, customer needs, financial goals, and cultural alignment.

For Mid-Level Leaders – When working with your team of leaders, be sure to rank strategic options based on their alignment with the vision, potential impact on vision attainment, and implementation feasibility. This will help prioritize which options to pursue and teach others the importance of aligning decision-making with strategic intent.

For Supervisory-Level Leaders – Ensure that your staffers understand how their work aligns with the vision and how their roles contribute to its achievement.

Idea Crosswalk

- **Leadership Mindset** – Well-designed decision selection screens can strengthen a firm's commitment to the strategic vision by placing it "front and center" in the decision-making process.
- **Company Culture** – Strategy-centered decision-making encourages the establishment of an organizational culture that is aligned with the vision of the enterprise.
- **People and Talent** – Decision-making frameworks that require strategic alignment simplify matters for new employees. Leaders joining the organization become productive more quickly when they understand how to prioritize choice among a variety of options.
- **Trust and Empowerment** – Trust and empowerment are enabled as staffers begin to adopt common decision-making practices.
- **Change Management** – When decision-making processes are aligned with the strategy, it becomes easier to introduce and manage changes required for effective execution.

Vision requires action; otherwise, it's just fantasy!

Master the art of execution, and you'll fast-track your journey to success!

Guru Guidance

Keep a close eye on your execution of the work needed to realize your vision and make adjustments along the way to ensure people are positioned to perform at their best.

Indeed, unleashing the full force and capabilities of the workforce is critical to achieving your strategic vision. When you tap into the diverse talents, skills, and passions of your people, you unlock a wellspring of creativity and dedication that propels the organization forward.

> *" . . . precision is a key to exceptional performance . . . "*

With that, putting the "right" people in the "right" roles is critical to vision attainment. After all, precision is a key to exceptional performance. So, positioning people in ways that enable them to operate as a highly functioning team is essential.

Correspondingly, you must be clear when designating responsibilities and decision-making authority to your teams. Productivity suffers when staffers struggle to understand their duties and decision rights. So, remove all doubt and make everyone involved aware of their responsibilities and roles.

When individuals within a company are empowered, motivated, and aligned with a clear strategic vision, they become a formidable collective force capable of achieving remarkable results.

How to Put It into Action

For Executive-Level Leaders – Require your team members to identify the projects and programs needed to realize the vision, and then charge them with getting those initiatives done.

DOI: 10.4324/9781003422754-33

For **Mid-Level Leaders** – Guide your team in defining their responsibilities in delivering on the work needed to successfully execute the action plans identified by the senior leadership team.

For **Supervisory-Level Leaders** – It is critical that your people grasp the company's direction and realize the crucial role that they play in propelling the business forward. Be sure to message this on a regular basis so your staffers appreciate how important they are to the enterprise's success.

Idea Crosswalk

- **Leadership Mindset** – Gaining employee commitment to the vision is the cornerstone of sustainable success.
- **Company Culture** – A solid action orientation shapes the development of a vibrant, forward-thinking culture that can perform in the short-term and will thrive in the long run.
- **People and Talent** – When an organization taps into the full potential of its workforce, it amplifies its chances of realizing its strategic goals.
- **Trust and Empowerment** – Pushing for steady advancement towards the goals set forth in the vision cultivates a sense of ownership and commitment among employees – and greater commitment translates into a deeper sense of trust within an organization.
- **Change Management** – The unrelenting pursuit of progress can lead to a change management philosophy that recognizes strategic advancement as a continuous journey that has no final finish line.

Relentlessly look for ways to expand and breathe new life into the strategic plan

Strategic planning should be viewed as a continuous process that keeps the strategic plan aligned with the organization's evolution over time.

Guru Guidance

Leaders can make strategic planning a continuous process by putting resources behind its "care and feeding."

Businesses constantly change. As such, their strategic plans need to change, too.

> *"Businesses constantly change. As such, their strategic plans need to change, too."*

Hence, it's important to make sure that strategic planning becomes a regular, ongoing process that is not resigned to being a once-a-year, budgeting exercise.

After all, the business landscape is rapidly changing, driven by external forces including technological advances, new market entrants, and changes in consumer preferences. By continuously seeking ways to improve and innovate and incorporating these ideas in the strategic plan, an organization can stay ahead of the competition.

An ongoing strategic planning process better enables organizations to swiftly adjust to these changes – a capability that an annual planning process just does not provide.

How to Put It into Action

For Executive-Level Leaders – Establish a regular schedule (on at least a quarterly basis) for reviewing the strategic plan with your team. Annual reviews are not enough to keep the plan and its associated projects top-of-mind.

DOI: 10.4324/9781003422754-34

For Mid-Level Leaders – Contribute to extending and revitalizing the strategic plan by identifying alternatives to the current strategic plan by taking stock of any new opportunities and challenges that crop up as your team goes about executing its work. Bring those ideas forward in reviews with senior leadership.

For Supervisory-Level Leaders – Make it a regular practice to step back from the day-to-day routine and look at the business from an outsider's perspective. As you do, identify opportunities that might be worth further consideration and offer those to your next-level leaders.

Idea Crosswalk

- **Leadership Mindset** – Leaders must lead by example and demonstrate their commitment to continuous strategic planning by driving the process throughout the year.
- **Company Culture** – Making strategic planning a continuous process brings about a culture of adaptability and agility, at the same time encouraging experimentation and a willingness to pivot, when necessary.
- **People and Talent** – When leaders think beyond achieving immediate goals and focus on the organization's long-term success, they cultivate strategic thinking with their staffers, too.
- **Trust and Empowerment** – By keeping the entire organization informed about the progress of the strategic plan and any changes made leaders can create the kind of transparency that fosters buy-in and commitment from their people.
- **Change Management** – When strategic planning becomes an ongoing and dynamic process it helps the organization navigate change and thrive in an ever-evolving business landscape.

Peer into the future by adopting scenario planning

Scenario planning provides organizations with a means to anticipate the future and determine how best to manage it, should a given situation arise.

Guru Guidance

When a crisis or unexpected event does happen, organizations that have engaged in scenario planning can make decisions more quickly. So, embracing the concept is worth the effort of instituting it.

Scenario planning is an approach that involves creating and analyzing multiple hypothetical scenarios or future situations. By examining different scenarios, organizations can develop strategies and contingency plans tailored to each possible future.

> *" . . . scenario planning helps reduce future uncertainties by providing a structured framework for considering various possibilities."*

In effect, scenario planning helps reduce future uncertainties by providing a structured framework for considering various possibilities. This, in turn, allows organizations to make more informed decisions when confronted with an emerging challenge.

The fact that stakeholders, including employees, customers, and potential investors often have more confidence in organizations that engage in scenario planning is only a bonus. In most cases, they see it as a sign of proactive risk management and responsible leadership.

By folding scenario planning into an organization's strategic planning process, leaders are better equipped to respond to unforeseen events and challenges, ultimately enhancing the firm's resilience and competitive edge in an ever-changing world.

DOI: 10.4324/9781003422754-35

How to Put It into Action

For Executive-Level Leaders – Fold scenario planning into your strategic planning processes. It presents the opportunity to uncover and consider strategic questions that would routinely be overlooked otherwise.

For Mid-Level Leaders – Dedicate time to defining early indicators that your team of leaders can use to identify and track before a scenario emerges that could do damage to your business before it even knows what hit it.

For Supervisory-Level Leaders – Supervisors play a vital role in implementing strategies and responses to various scenarios. Strive to understand the scenario plans and share this understanding with your team so that they become aware of the steps they will be asked to take to confront emerging threats to the enterprise.

Idea Crosswalk

- **Leadership Mindset** – Organizations that use scenario planning can gain a competitive advantage by being better positioned to seize opportunities that arise in uncertain times – a sure sign of proactive leadership.
- **Company Culture** – By envisioning a range of scenarios, organizations can pinpoint potential threats that might otherwise have been overlooked, improving the cultural resiliency of the enterprise.
- **People and Talent** – A leadership team that contemplates what it will need to confront potential scenarios tends to seek improvements in its talent pool. After all, staffers must be prepared to handle the unexpected.
- **Trust and Empowerment** – By identifying risks and vulnerabilities in advance, organizations can take proactive steps to mitigate those risks, enhancing employee trust in their leadership.
- **Change Management** – Organizations that regularly practice scenario planning are often more adaptable and agile in the face of change.

Leadership Tip 33

Your vision story must include a captivating picture of your ideal culture

A work setting is characterized by its culture. Make your culture appealing and you will attract top talent from around the globe.

Guru Guidance

Ask your team to describe the specific behaviors, interactions, and outcomes they would like to see take shape in the future. Add those workplace culture ideas to the organization's vision story.

When people can see and imagine the kind of culture that they want to be part of, they are more likely to feel inspired and motivated to work towards creating it. So, how do we craft a captivating picture of your desired company culture in a vision story?

> *"You can begin by describing a company culture where leaders talk about the greater purpose . . . "*

You can begin by describing a workplace where leaders talk about the greater purpose, staff feel duty-bound to do their jobs at the highest level (so as not to let their teammates down), and people are encouraged to venture out of their comfort zones in order to bring better thinking to the table.

Indeed, a well-crafted discussion of the target workplace culture provides clarity on what the organization is striving to cultivate. It helps employees understand the expectations and norms, reducing ambiguity and fostering a shared understanding of the desired work environment.

In time, you will begin to attract like-minded individuals to the vision adoption effort. Once a critical mass forms, the force for change will be so great that the culture can't help but improve, too.

DOI: 10.4324/9781003422754-36

How to Put It into Action

For Executive-Level Leaders – Begin to discuss with your team of leaders what the "perfect" workplace culture looks like – incorporate those ideas into the vision for the enterprise.

For Mid-Level Leaders – Use visual aids, metaphors, or symbols to represent the ideal culture. These can make the vision more vivid and accessible. Consider creating a vision board that represents the target culture.

For Supervisory-Level Leaders – Ask your team members to share their personal values. Discuss how these values align with the organization's cultural vision, emphasizing how, by working together, they will create a workplace that they can be proud of.

Idea Crosswalk

- **Leadership Mindset** – An emphasis on culture serves to drive change in the way that staffers behave as they work to achieve the vision.
- **Company Culture** – Describing the desired culture is an essential part of vision storytelling. A leader would be remiss not to cover it in their strategic vision work.
- **People and Talent** – People want to understand how they "fit" into the vision and discussing culture helps them to "see" where they can play a meaningful role in the organization's future.
- **Trust and Empowerment** – Staffers won't give their best effort to achieve the vision if the culture is not accommodating and aligned with their personal values.
- **Change Management** – The cultural discussion found in most vision stories frames many of the changes an organization must tackle to achieve its strategic ambitions.

Leadership Tip 34

Your strategies are only as good as their cultural alignment

Cultural "fit" is needed for strategies to deliver on their promises.

Guru Guidance

In essence, the success of a strategy depends on its integration with the cultural fabric of the organization. When strategies are developed and implemented with cultural alignment in mind, they are more likely to be embraced and lead to better overall outcomes for the enterprise.

Culture heavily influences how strategies are executed and implemented. If a strategy is in conflict with a company's prevailing culture or operating models, it will face resistance from staffers and not be effectively executed.

On the other hand, strategies that align with the culture are more likely to be embraced and carried out by employees. When employees believe in the strategy and understand how it supports the organization's culture, they will actively support and champion its success.

> *" . . . strategies that align with the culture are more likely to be embraced and carried out by employees."*

As such, strategies, aligned with a company's culture, foster innovation and creativity among the workforce. Because of better buy-in, staffers are more eager to discover innovative ways to implement the strategy, too. This, in turn, inspires confidence that the strategies will deliver the desired results.

Similarly, strategies that are in cultural alignment reinforce and strengthen the organization's identity and purpose in the marketplace. Customers and other key stakeholders are attracted to this sense of unity and purpose.

DOI: 10.4324/9781003422754-37

How to Put It into Action

For Executive-Level Leaders – Create a framework or assessment tool to evaluate potential strategies for their alignment with the company's culture. This can help leaders objectively assess whether a proposed strategy is a good fit.

For Mid-Level Leaders – Engage employees at all levels in the strategy development process. Seek their input, ideas, and feedback on how the strategy can align with the company culture. Their involvement can inspire a sense of ownership and commitment to the strategy.

For Supervisory-Level Leaders – When leading key strategic initiatives assess how each critical decision point aligns with the company's culture and values. Choose the options that align the best.

Idea Crosswalk

- **Leadership Mindset** – The commitment to aligning strategies with culture fosters faith in leadership.
- **Company Culture** – Proper strategic and cultural alignment reinforces an enterprise's workplace purpose.
- **People and Talent** – Strong cultural alignment results in talent development efforts that emphasize cultural fit, helping employees grow within the organization while preserving cultural integrity.
- **Trust and Empowerment** – Strategies aligned with culture builds trust and credibility among employees, customers, and stakeholders.
- **Change Management** – Culture-aligned strategies are more likely to be accepted by employees during times of change.

Part III

Company Culture Tips

Indispensable leaders don't leave their company culture to chance. Rather, they reset and enrich it purposefully with their people and customers in mind.

They know that company culture determines the preferred way of execution and achievement within an organization. An exceptional leader will take it upon themselves to align the culture with their vision for the future.

Leaders drive cultural change to become indispensable to their customers. It is the customer who decides if an organization is one that can't be lived without. Consequently, the culture must be deliberately "designed" in ways that enable staff to delight the customer.

These tips help leaders to recast their company culture to ensure that their organizations are "of choice" within the markets that they serve.

DOI: 10.4324/9781003422754-38

Winning starts with culture

Culture is the foundation upon which an organization's success is built.

Guru Guidance

A winning organization needs its people to adopt a winning mindset. Despite a leader's best efforts, without it, there's no way a positive and healthy culture can emerge.

"Winning starts with culture" is a widely recognized principle in business and organizational management. This concept emphasizes that a positive and healthy company culture is a fundamental prerequisite for achieving success and winning in the marketplace.

> *"This concept emphasizes that a positive and healthy organizational culture is a fundamental prerequisite for achieving success and winning in the marketplace."*

Of course, a winning culture must be cultivated and reinforced through strong leadership. Effective leaders set the tone for the organization, inspiring and guiding their teams to develop the mindset needed to achieve success.

Additionally, organizations with a strong and success-driven culture are more likely to attract top talent and retain the "right" people required to remain on top of their competitors.

Further, there's little doubt that when employees share a common purpose and values, they will work diligently together to accomplish the desired results. A strong culture acts as the glue that keeps people focused on achieving common goals.

But please note, winning is not just about making short-term gains; it's also about achieving continual success. A culture that embodies all of the attributes required to promote winning behavior is absolutely essential to the long-term success of the enterprise.

DOI: 10.4324/9781003422754-39

How to Put It into Action

For Executive-Level Leaders – Readily make mid-course adjustments. Be willing to adapt and evolve the culture as the organization grows and changes. A winning culture should be flexible and responsive.

For Mid-Level Leaders – Provide coaching and mentoring to your team of next-level leaders to help them develop the skills and attitudes that align with the winning culture.

For Supervisory-Level Leaders – Promptly address behaviors that go against the desired culture. Leaders should not tolerate actions that undermine a positive work environment.

Idea Crosswalk

- **Leadership Mindset** – Leaders who foster a winning culture set an example by embodying the desired values and behaviors needed to sustain a winning team, reinforcing the spirit that strong, supportive, and effective leadership brings to an organization.
- **Vision** – A winning culture must be closely aligned with the organization's vision. After all, culture enables an enterprise to flourish.
- **People and Talent** – A success-driven culture envelopes high achievers and gives them a sense of belonging, engagement, and common identity – all critical elements of winning in the marketplace.
- **Trust and Empowerment** – When a team wins together, they learn the true meaning of being mutually dependent on one another. Trust is a natural byproduct of a winning culture.
- **Change Management** – Employees working in a winning organization are more adaptable, open to change, and willing to embrace it. They know that business success is worth the effort required to overcome the challenges that come with change.

Culture is nothing more than the way your people behave

Don't add confusion to the mix by overthinking the definition.

Guru Guidance

Too many leaders avoid taking charge of shaping company culture because they are unclear about what culture means or how it's shaped. The best place to begin is by simply observing employee behavior. When you do, the steps required to drive culture change become readily apparent.

The culture of an organization is principally influenced by the shared attitudes, values, and behaviors of its workforce.

Because culture is a social phenomenon (i.e., consider what is meant by Aztec culture, Ancient Egyptian culture, etc.), even in a workplace context, company culture is nothing more than the product of the interactions among, and conduct of, staff members.

> *"When leaders uphold the cultural values, employees are more likely to follow suit. When they don't, staffers won't, either."*

Of course, leadership plays a significant role in shaping and swaying company culture. A leader's behavior influences the behaviors of the people whom they lead. Thus, it's a game of follow the leader. When leaders uphold cultural values, employees are more likely to follow suit. When they don't, staffers won't, either.

With that, employees form their perceptions of the company culture based on what they observe and experience daily. When they see their colleagues consistently behaving in a certain way and experiencing positive or negative consequences as a result, it impacts their own behavior.

Over time, certain behaviors become entrenched as cultural norms and traditions. For example, if teamwork and collaboration are valued, employees will tend to work together and support one another. If innovation is a priority, employees will exhibit behaviors that encourage creative thinking and problem-solving.

DOI: 10.4324/9781003422754-40

So, don't overthink it. Just know that you can shape-shift culture by changing the behavior of people in the company.

How to Put It into Action

For Executive-Level Leaders – Be sure that you identify desired workplace behaviors and attitudes, fully describe each one, and, most importantly, communicate them regularly.

For Mid-Level Leaders – Recognize that company culture is not static; it evolves over time. Work to help your leaders make the changes in the culture you want to create by focusing them on behavioral change.

For Supervisory-Level Leaders – Your people learn from each other. Be sure to reinforce the behaviors in individuals that you want repeated.

Idea Crosswalk

- **Leadership Mindset** – When positive behaviors are encouraged and negative behaviors are addressed, a healthy and vibrant company culture emerges. Leaders must decide to set the tone.
- **Vision** – Culture is built upon shared values, beliefs, and norms that employees hold. Those ideas should be spelled out in your vision story.
- **People and Talent** – Engaged employees will embody and promote desired cultural behaviors – making them enthusiastic ambassadors of the culture.
- **Trust and Empowerment** – To establish a high-trust organization that enables its people to achieve, leaders must adopt empowering behaviors.
- **Change Management** – Positive behaviors, such as teamwork and collaboration, strengthen any change effort.

Culture must be built by design, or your business will falter

It is your company culture that will determine if your strategies are achievable.

Guru Guidance

Don't leave your culture to chance. Instead, deliberately design your company culture in support of your strategic pursuits.

> " . . . *even if your business strategy is exceptional; it will falter without an organizational culture that fosters the execution of that strategy.*"

Most of us have heard the adage: "culture eats strategy for breakfast." It is often attributed to Peter Drucker, though no credible citation exists that proves he was the originator of the idea.

Nonetheless, this tip borrows from the spirit of the expression, which suggests even if your business strategies are exceptional, they will falter without an organizational culture that fosters the execution of those strategies.

After all, while a well-crafted business strategy is essential, it remains just a paper plan without proper execution. Culture plays a pivotal role in enabling or hindering the successful implementation of a strategy.

Remember, culture ultimately drives employee behavior. A positive culture promotes collaboration, innovation, and commitment, while a negative culture can lead to apathy, resistance, and conflict.

Clearly, organizations need positive cultures to consistently win in the marketplace.

DOI: 10.4324/9781003422754-41

How to Put It into Action

For **Executive-Level Leaders** – Regularly articulate the core values and principles that underpin the desired culture and ensure these are integrated into the company's mission statements and vision stories.

For **Mid-Level Leaders** – Invest in training and development programs that help employees understand and adopt behaviors that further the institutionalization of the desired culture.

For **Supervisory-Level Leaders** – Ensure that, during the onboarding process, new employees receive an orientation program that reinforces the company's culture.

Idea Crosswalk

- **Leadership Mindset** – Leaders must prioritize both strategy and culture development to ensure the long-term success of their enterprises.
- **Vision** – A strong and vibrant organizational culture is not just nice to have; it's a fundamental driver of success.
- **People and Talent** – A distinctive and positive culture can be a source of competitive advantage. It attracts top talent, enhances customer relationships, and separates a company from its competitors.
- **Trust and Empowerment** – When employees work in organizations with strong cultures, they are more likely to make choices in support of achieving long-term goals – this behavior contributes to extending trust within an enterprise.
- **Change Management** – Solid company culture encourages alignment with the strategy. So, employees are more likely to work together on needed change initiatives to achieve their shared goals.

Culture can kill great ideas, if you let it!

Don't limit your solution to what was accepted in the past.

Guru Guidance

Leaders often prefer to stick with what they know, even when those approaches are proving to be no longer effective. This stifles creativity and prevents great ideas from gaining traction. Remember tremendous opportunities avail themselves to you when you break through your comfort zone.

Radical solutions to complex problems can often be discovered when we challenge ourselves by asking: "Why not?" Why not use different approaches to problem-solving? Why not try new ideas? Why not do something different?

> " . . . *cultivate a culture that values out-of-the-box thinking* . . . "

Potentially groundbreaking concepts are left on the drawing board in organizations that have cultures that prioritize conformity and consensus, where employees are rewarded for maintaining peace and agreement and not for developing a capacity to critically evaluate new ideas. Don't let that happen in your organization!

Instead, cultivate a culture that values out-of-the-box thinking, encourages risk-taking, supports experimentation, fosters collaboration, and provides the necessary resources and incentives for employees to innovate.

The highly competitive landscape today requires regular refinement and improvement to the products and services that an enterprise offers – it's the only way to retain and capture market share.

How to Put It into Action

For Executive-Level Leaders – Cultivate a culture that promotes critical thinking and the acceptance of new ideas by allocating resources in

DOI: 10.4324/9781003422754-42

support of breakthrough concepts, even when those concepts are quite different from anything pursued by the organization in the past.

For Mid-Level Leaders – A culture that encourages collaboration and inter-disciplinary thinking is more likely to nurture great ideas. To enable this, seek to break down organizational silos that often foster conformity of thinking. Replace the silo mentality with one that encourages cooperation and collaboration across functional areas within the enterprise.

For Supervisory-Level Leaders – Staffers will be reluctant to propose new ideas in organizational cultures that punish failure. Help your people break through this limiting mindset by asking them for input on better ways to operate.

Idea Crosswalk

- **Leadership Mindset** – Leaders must reduce the "groupthink" that often stifles breakthrough thinking and work to establish a learning culture that seeks to steadily improve.
- **Vision** – A vision should describe the communication infrastructure that enables good ideas to percolate up to top decision-makers (who can provide the backing needed to pilot and develop breakthrough concepts).
- **People and Talent** – A culture that does not recognize and reward innovation can "turn off" employees and limit their willingness to propose or champion great ideas.
- **Trust and Empowerment** – Decision-making processes may be slow, and ideas can get bogged down in layers of approval, making it difficult for them to see the light of day. Empowering staffers to make the call enables breakthrough thinking.
- **Change Management** – Resistance to change plays a major role in why great ideas are often knocked down by company culture. Change management frameworks need to take this into account and offer ways to overcome change resistance.

Leadership voids will always be filled

When there is a lack of leadership, people often feel a sense of uncertainty and will begin to follow whoever steps up – even if that person heads in the wrong direction.

Guru Guidance

We have a natural inclination to seek information, clarity, and direction. Be sure your culture is designed to provide the formal leadership that individuals seek or risk others influencing how your people behave.

The filling of leadership voids is a natural human response to the need for clarity, direction, and understanding. In the absence of clear leadership, individuals often attempt to regain a sense of control by trying to make sense of unclear situations through rumors and perceived innuendo. In other words, in a work setting where information is lacking, any "dot" can (and will) be connected. It's just what we do.

> *" . . . as leaders, we must step up and lead the way . . . "*

Indeed, people inherently dislike ambiguity and uncertainty. When leadership does not provide clear guidance or information, individuals seek to fill the void with their own interpretations and assumptions, and that's not the kind of culture one wants to cultivate. It creates cognitive dissonance and brings chaos to the workplace.

Additionally, we often look to authority figures for guidance and direction, particularly in the context of work or group dynamics. When leadership is absent, people may look to themselves or others to take on unofficial leadership roles and provide direction. All bets are off when this is allowed to happen. Instead, as leaders, we must step up and lead the way.

DOI: 10.4324/9781003422754-43

How to Put It into Action

For Executive-Level Leaders – Mitigate potential cultural problems by providing clear communication, guidance, and support, reducing the tendency for people to fill the void with rumors and speculation.

For Mid-Level Leaders – Encourage your team of leaders to take ownership of their work and make decisions within their scope of responsibility.

For Supervisory-Level Leaders – Demonstrate strong leadership by being present, involving your people in problem-solving, and making the call when a decision is needed.

Idea Crosswalk

- **Leadership Mindset** – Leaders need to be approachable and available to their people, encouraging open and honest communication by actively listening and offering appropriate feedback.
- **Vision** – A vision must include ideas about leaders creating an environment where leadership voids are minimized, and employees are motivated, engaged, and confident.
- **People and Talent** – Leaders need training, coaching, and opportunities for skills enhancement to ensure they have the knowledge and tools needed to excel in their leadership roles, so no voids develop.
- **Trust and Empowerment** – Implementing feedback channels where employees can express their concerns, ideas, and suggestions enables leaders to act on and address issues promptly, which helps trust grow in the workplace.
- **Change Management** – Preventing leadership voids during change pursuits is crucial for maintaining a healthy and productive work environment.

Weak leadership always wreaks havoc

Without a strong sense of direction, employees may become disoriented and lack motivation, leading to a lack of focus and alignment within the organization.

Guru Guidance

Effective communication is crucial for an organization's success. Weak leaders struggle to convey important information, expectations, and feedback clearly, leading to misunderstandings, confusion, and a breakdown in performance. Work to be an exceptional leader!

Strong leadership is essential for an organization's success and long-term viability. Weak leadership, on the other hand, creates chaos and needless drama within an enterprise.

> *"Employees become disengaged and demotivated when they do not trust their leaders to effectively lead them."*

Moreover, weak leaders fail to inspire and motivate their teams. Employees become disengaged and demotivated when they do not trust their leaders to effectively lead them.

Further, poor morale kills productivity and contributes to higher turnover rates – leading to a culture of complacency, where employees do not take responsibility for their work or outcomes.

In the end, it's nearly impossible to do our best work within a rudderless work setting. Weak leadership erodes trust and brings about inconsistency, bias, and always, poor performance, which has a negative impact on the company's bottom line.

How to Put It into Action

For Executive-Level Leaders – Develop your leaders or move them out.

Training, coaching, and mentorship programs can help weaker leaders

DOI: 10.4324/9781003422754-44

improve their skills and competencies. However, if they lack the ability to lead and inspire others, they must be jettisoned. The risk to the business is too great to tolerate poor leadership anywhere in the organization.

For Mid-Level Leaders – Begin to have difficult conversations with any weaker leaders on your team, addressing their shortcomings and suggesting ways to improve. They need constructive and honest feedback to stand any chance of becoming better leaders.

For Supervisory-Level Leaders – Hold your people accountable for their actions and decisions. Some may be considered for future leadership opportunities, and they need to recognize that leaders lead by being responsible to the people whom they lead.

Idea Crosswalk

- **Leadership Mindset** – Leaders must hold colleagues to a high standard of excellence.
- **Vision** – Strong leadership teams are simply better at communicating an organization's vision and strategies to the workforce. Staffers need that clarity to perform at their best.
- **People and Talent** – It takes effective leaders to handle conflicts and challenges within their teams, which, in turn, leads to better business results.
- **Trust and Empowerment** – Stronger leaders offer greater transparency in decision-making, promoting trust in their ability to navigate change effectively and make decisions that benefit the entire organization.
- **Change Management** – A competent leadership team is more adaptable in the face of change. In fact, they embrace it, guiding their teams through transitions with confidence.

Encourage people to speak their minds!

Staffers must be invited to offer dissenting opinions so the best ideas can be considered.

Guru Guidance

Stomp out "Group Think," a phenomenon where group members conform to a consensus view without critical evaluation, by using this idea at your next team meeting.

Want to improve outcomes at your company? Encourage your employees to disagree with you. It is really the only way to get the best answers on the table and to build the team-based environment required to win.

What's more, promoting the notion that your team has an obligation to speak up when they see a better way to get things done not only improves your results and enhances your company culture, but it recasts the concept of *dissent* as a *duty* that is part of the job requirement.

> *" . . . it recasts the concept of dissent as a duty that is part of the job requirement."*

Truly, welcoming differing points of view signals to your people that it's acceptable for them to speak their minds in the spirit of discovering the best path forward for the enterprise.

How to Put It into Action

For Executive-Level Leaders – Let it be known that you find it absolutely acceptable for team members to push back against your ideas if they have a better one. Show that you're looking for the best idea, not looking for a blind, sycophantic agreement with you.

For Mid-Level Leaders – When discussing alternatives, it is likely that some opposing ideas will lack merit right out of the box. When this happens, use it as an opportunity to give your team of leaders feedback

DOI: 10.4324/9781003422754-45

and teach them why those ideas may not work in practice. This way, they get stronger and learn through your experience and guidance.

For Supervisory-Level Leaders – Publicly acknowledge and thank team members who offer dissenting opinions. Express appreciation for their willingness to speak up and contribute to better decision-making.

Idea Crosswalk

- **Leadership Mindset** – Top leaders should encourage regular dialogue, ask open-ended questions, and provide opportunities for team members to share their thoughts and concerns.
- **Vision** – The best vision stories describe work settings where staffers feel safe to express dissent without fear of retribution or criticism.
- **People and Talent** – Speaking one's mind can be an organizational norm that indicates to your people that they are expected to contribute their "best thinking" for the good of the enterprise.
- **Trust and Empowerment** – Taking action on the feedback received, when appropriate, demonstrates that leadership values employee input. In time, this grows trust within the organization.
- **Change Management** – A strong change management framework includes regularly asking key stakeholders for feedback on their concerns, ideas, or alternative viewpoints.

Account for the next generation ethos when reimagining the culture

If company culture does not align with the values and expectations of the next generation of staffers, they may seek employment elsewhere.

Guru Guidance

There's no doubt that when employees feel understood and valued by their employer, they are more likely to become engaged and motivated with the work at hand. Consider this when constructing your company culture for the future.

Recognize that many of today's younger employees will be the leaders of tomorrow. Fostering a culture that supports their ideals and beliefs only serves to engage and inspire them to give their best effort to their jobs. Their commitment to the organization only grows as more opportunities come their way and they move along in their careers.

> *"Recognize that many of today's younger employees will be the leaders of tomorrow."*

Further, a company's reputation and brand image are influenced by its culture and how it aligns with societal values, too. A culture that reflects the next generation ethos enhances a company's image and appeal to customers, investors, and partners, alike.

With that, gaining the necessary perspective and understanding of these future generations of staffers can be daunting. So, it is wise to consider seeking advice from "future of work" experts who specialize in next-generation trends and culture, as they can provide valuable insights and guidance.

With this added awareness, today's top leaders can be sure to incorporate cultural changes that matter to the next generation.

DOI: 10.4324/9781003422754-46

How to Put It into Action

For Executive-Level Leaders – Begin by thoroughly researching and understanding the values, beliefs, and expectations of the next generation in your workforce and the target talent market. This may involve surveys, focus groups, and staying up-to-date with societal trends.

For Mid-Level Leaders – It is always helpful to include younger employees in any company culture redesign efforts. Form cross-generational teams to brainstorm ideas, develop initiatives, and implement changes.

For Supervisory-Level Leaders – Actively engage with younger employees and stakeholders to listen to their apprehensions, ideas, and feedback. Encourage open and transparent communication where they feel comfortable sharing their perspectives with you.

Idea Crosswalk

- **Leadership Mindset** – Top leaders need to consider some of the cultural characteristics that next generation staffers are looking for including flexible work arrangements, opportunities for skill development, and a greater emphasis on work-life integration.
- **Vision** – The vision story should clearly and consistently cover the organization's commitment to the next generation ethos.
- **People and Talent** – Younger employees often seek opportunities for advancement and development. It's essential that Talent Development programs provide clear paths for career progression and growth within the organization.
- **Trust and Empowerment** – Trust grows in organizations that regularly assess how well it is supporting the next generation mindset and values.
- **Change Management** – Change processes must encourage collaboration and cross-functional teamwork, which include the younger generations of employees.

Your people need to see their own success in your vision

If they can imagine being part of it and personally succeeding, you will engage them in the process of making it a reality.

Guru Guidance

Once the vision is socialized, encourage your leaders to delegate authority and responsibility whenever feasible, allowing team members to take ownership of the vision as they do their work.

Vision achievement doesn't happen by magic. It transpires every day through the choices and actions of everyone in the organization.

> *"Everybody must come to understand how their efforts contribute to propelling the company forward."*

That said, it serves as a powerful motivator when individuals see their personal success as part of a larger vision. This insight enhances their sense of purpose and engagement with the work at hand.

As important, staffers are more likely to invest time and energy into a vision when they feel a personal stake in its realization. This sense of ownership leads to a stronger commitment to overcoming challenges and doing what is needed to succeed.

Additionally, your people are more likely to seek opportunities for learning and development, aiming not only to meet current work demands but also to cultivate additional capabilities in order to better contribute to achieving strategic goals.

Undoubtedly, our job as leaders is to help our team members understand what is in it for them and how they can take specific actions within their areas of responsibility to enable its achievement.

DOI: 10.4324/9781003422754-47

How to Put It into Action

For Executive-Level Leaders – Make vision achievement a part of your monthly meetings with direct reports. Hold your people accountable for driving new behaviors into the organization.

For Mid-Level Leaders – Demonstrate the kinds of proactive behavior that you want your leaders to bring to their teams. Whenever possible, strike up conversations with them about their career aspirations and how they can develop skills to achieve those personal goals.

For Supervisory-Level Leaders – Facilitate a discussion with your team to help them translate the vision into "actionable" steps that they can take to incorporate vision achievement into what they do every day in their jobs – showing them what they can gain by helping the team achieve its goals.

Idea Crosswalk

- **Leadership Mindset** – It is a leader's job to reinforce the vision and help people relate to it at an emotional level.
- **Vision** – The culture must align with the vision. It happens through shifts in the behavior of leadership and staff alike.
- **People and Talent** – The vision must engage and inspire, or no one will work to achieve it. Helping people to associate their personal success with business success serves to inspire their commitment to the cause.
- **Trust and Empowerment** – The vision needs to promote the idea of staffer autonomy in the pursuit of common goals. This will lead to greater trust and enable the empowerment of staff to do the "right" things.
- **Change Management** – People need to connect the goals of a given change initiative with the overall vision for the enterprise. When in alignment, change efforts tend to move more swiftly to completion.

Take difficulties in stride and watch how your people respond

Leaders who handle difficulties with composure and grace demonstrate what good looks like.

Guru Guidance

When leaders handle challenges calmly and confidently, they serve as role models for their employees. In turn, this encourages employees to develop their own resilience, which leads to more constructive and adaptive approaches to challenges.

Leaders who view difficulties as opportunities for growth and learning inspire employees to adopt a similar mindset. This can lead to a culture where employees are more open to learning from challenges and view setbacks as stepping stones to improvement.

Also, the simple act of witnessing a leader successfully tackling difficulties boosts a staff's confidence in their own abilities. Employees are more likely to take on challenges and believe in their own capacity to overcome them when they see their leaders doing the same.

> *" . . . leadership adaptability is proving to be a critical skill . . . "*

Similarly, leaders who handle difficulties with grace and adaptability encourage their staffers to be more flexible, too. In a rapidly changing work environment, leadership adaptability is proving to be a critical skill – one that separates success from failure.

To be sure, staff members often look to their leaders for guidance during difficult times. When leaders handle difficulties with confidence, employee anxieties diminish and they gain a stronger sense of stability and security.

Leaders, who demonstrate that they can handle challenges with poise, inspire confidence and trust, and set a positive example for how to effectively overcome difficulties. So, keep your cool under pressure. Your people are watching!

DOI: 10.4324/9781003422754-48

How to Put It into Action

For Executive-Level Leaders – Make decisions decisively and communicate them with confidence. Even if decisions are difficult, displaying conviction in your choices can inspire trust and commitment among staff members.

For Mid-Level Leaders – Focus on identifying and implementing solutions rather than dwelling on the problem. This pragmatic approach inspires confidence and motivates your team of leaders.

For Supervisory-Level Leaders – Provide support and encouragement to your team throughout the toughest of times. Recognize their efforts and celebrate small victories, even in the face of ongoing challenges.

Idea Crosswalk

- **Leadership Mindset** – Demonstrating composure, resilience, and confidence in the face of challenges exemplifies a solid leadership mentality centered on strength, adaptability, and a commitment to problem-solving.
- **Vision** – By keeping their focus on the vision, leaders inspire a sense of purpose and direction among their team members, even in the midst of difficulties.
- **People and Talent** – The emphasis on collaboration and transparency in addressing challenges can foster a sense of belonging and teamwork among employees.
- **Trust and Empowerment** – Trust is essential for maintaining a positive attitude among team members during hard business times.
- **Change Management** – Handling challenges with aplomb often involves adapting to new circumstances, adjusting strategies, and making important decisions. These actions are central to any change activities within an organization.

Leadership Tip 45

Resiliency can be taught

Resilient people make resilient cultures.

Guru Guidance

A resilient culture is built one person at a time. So, be sure to regularly provide your people with the training and coaching that they need to become more resilient.

> " ... *staffers must learn the mental techniques and actions needed for protecting themselves* ... "

Resilience is a critical cultural attribute for every organization. It serves as the foundational element that enables an organization to more effectively anticipate, prepare for, respond to, and adapt in the face of escalating market disruptions, changing customer demands, and external competitive forces that can potentially destabilize a business.

For these reasons, staffers must learn the mental techniques and actions needed to protect themselves from the potential negative effects of everyday stressors that arise from their work and personal lives.

This can be achieved through the provision of proper coaching and training of the kind that promotes the adoption of healthy mental, physical, social, and spirit-feeding behaviors, which make people stronger in the face of setbacks.

When properly trained in the behaviors that enhance resilience, a community of resilient leaders emerges – it is these communities that will shape-shift the culture into one that can take adversity in stride.

DOI: 10.4324/9781003422754-49

How to Put It into Action

For Executive-Level Leaders – Make resources available to support employees' mental and emotional well-being, such as access to counseling services, wellness programs, and flexible work arrangements.

For Mid-Level Leaders – Conduct regular one-on-one meetings with employees to check on their well-being, discuss workload, and address any concerns or challenges they may be facing.

For Supervisory-Level Leaders – Plan for your team's resiliency training. Adjust work schedules so that you can attend the training, too. Work to be the example that your people can follow by practicing what you've learned through these training sessions.

Idea Crosswalk

- **Leadership Mindset** – When leaders encourage staffers to prioritize self-care activities like exercise, healthy eating, and getting enough sleep, they enhance the overall resilience of the enterprise.
- **Vision** – Strategic vision stories should include a discussion of a culture that encourages open and transparent communication where employees feel comfortable discussing their challenges and seeking support when needed.
- **People and Talent** – A culture that encourages employees to take breaks, use vacation time, and disconnect from work outside of business hours leads to more organizational resilience.
- **Trust and Empowerment** – Adopting a supportive leadership style enhances trust and improves cultural resilience within an enterprise.
- **Change Management** – A strong support network can help individuals cope with the challenges that change brings. Indeed, change activities are better managed where a strong workplace community ideal exists.

Feed the spirit. It shapes a firm's values, principles, and purpose

A leader's ability to feed the spirit can have a profound impact on reshaping company culture.

Guru Guidance

Company culture is the behavior that comes from shared values, beliefs, and a single-mindedness that defines how an organization operates. When a leader focuses on nurturing and nourishing the spirits of their team members, transformative change occurs within the enterprise.

A leader's ability to feed the spirit of their team members can reshape company culture by creating a more positive, engaged, and supportive work environment. Establishing team rituals or traditions contributes to a shared identity and culture that serves to build the camaraderie needed for people to flourish.

When leaders demonstrate that they care about the well-being of their team members, they enhance employee engagement. Engaged employees are more connected to their work, enthusiastic about their roles, and committed to the organization's core mission.

> *" . . . a workplace culture that feeds the spirit leads to higher employee satisfaction and lower turnover rates."*

Indeed, trust and transparency is enhanced when leaders show enthusiasm, dedication, and a positive attitude toward their staffers. Employees feel more comfortable being who they are as they go about executing their daily tasks.

Further, a workplace culture that feeds the spirit leads to improved morale and lower turnover rates. Satisfied staffers are more likely to stay with the organization – reducing disruption (when key players leave) and lowering recruitment and training costs for the enterprise.

Remember, employees who are inspired and motivated are more likely to think outside the box, generate new ideas, and contribute to the organization's growth and adaptability!

DOI: 10.4324/9781003422754-50

How to Put It into Action

For Executive-Level Leaders – Promote initiatives that promote *esprit de corps* among employees, such as offsite retreats, team lunches, or even simple in-office social activities.

For Mid-Level Leaders – Encourage healthy work-life integration among your team of leaders, it is an easy way of showing them that you care about their well-being.

For Supervisory-Level Leaders – Organize regular team-building activities to strengthen interpersonal relationships among your team members.

Idea Crosswalk

- **Leadership Mindset** – When leaders feed the spirit of their team members, they tap into their intrinsic motivations and passions. This leads to increased engagement and a deeper sense of purpose among staffers.
- **Vision** – A motivated and engaged workforce is a key asset for achieving the organization's strategic goals.
- **People and Talent** – A greater sense of unity among staff members helps them to find meaning and fulfillment in their work. This sense of purpose can have a profound impact on job satisfaction and overall contentment.
- **Trust and Empowerment** – Be kind to your people and they will build trust in you!
- **Change Management** – Leaders build stronger, more resilient, and more innovative teams by addressing the emotional and motivational needs of their employees during times of change.

Take care of yourself – you need to be strong to help your team

It is fine to rest, when rest is needed. Just, don't give up!

Guru Guidance

No one is invincible. Take a break when you feel burn-out coming on.

Remember to be kind to yourself. Take the time to clear your head. It helps you to regain your composure. It helps you replenish your strength. You will become more resilient as a result.

> *"Taking time to restore your energy is always better than losing your cool . . . "*

Indeed, giving yourself permission to take a break is so very important. Taking time to restore your energy is always better than losing your cool – and doing, or saying, something that you will regret later.

Paradoxically, taking breaks can boost productivity and focus. Short, well-planned breaks can help leaders maintain concentration and prevent mental fatigue. Leaders who take breaks are more efficient and effective when they return to their tasks.

The fact is your team will benefit from this, as well. By taking care of yourself, you enhance your ability and willingness to take care of them.

After all, you are no good to anyone if you're burned out and mentally exhausted. Don't feel guilty about taking a break!

How to Put It into Action

For Executive-Level Leaders – Promote self-care as a company value by discussing it at company-wide events and by ensuring that it is reflected in your organization's vision story.

For Mid-Level Leaders – Set the example that you want your team of leaders to follow by taking breaks to replenish your energy and refuel your spirit to lead.

DOI: 10.4324/9781003422754-51

For Supervisory-Level Leaders – Set time aside during the day to recharge and reinvigorate yourself so that you can always bring your best to your team.

Idea Crosswalk

- **Leadership Mindset** – The idea that responsible leadership includes taking care of one's mental and physical health reinforces a culture of accountability and self-care among leaders.
- **Vision** – A strategic vision must prioritize employee well-being, which supports a healthier, more engaged, and motivated workforce.
- **People and Talent** – An organization that values self-care as part of a healthy work culture is more likely to attract and retain talent. Prospective employees are drawn to organizations that prioritize effective work-life integration.
- **Trust and Empowerment** – A leader who promotes a balanced work culture earns the trust of employees.
- **Change Management** – A focus on well-being and work-life integration during periods of change inspires employee engagement in those change efforts.

Practice tolerance by asking this simple question: *Is it worth it?*

Some arguments are not worth having.

Guru Guidance

An understanding leader boosts team morale by demonstrating fairness and respect. When team members perceive that their leader values them as people, it leads to higher job satisfaction and a stronger commitment to the organization.

The feeling of needing to defend one's turf is part of the human condition. In fact, it's the source of many armed conflicts around the globe. It is also fodder for much of the drama that transpires within the workplace today.

Sometimes we have no choice, but to dig in and defend our position. The cause is worth fighting for. Many times, though, the collateral damage that comes with the conflict is not worth the battle.

> *"The answer to this question can make all the difference ... "*

True wisdom comes when we can discern the difference between when it's wise to defend and when it's better to avoid intensifying a disagreement.

One of the ways in which leaders can develop the insight needed to gain this kind of wisdom is to take the time needed to ask one simple question: *"Is it worth it?"*

The answer to this question can make all the difference between you doing, or saying, something that you may regret later, or building a reputation as a mature and thoughtful leader over time. Learning to ask the question, is one of the ways you can develop the tolerance needed for leadership excellence.

DOI: 10.4324/9781003422754-52

How to Put It into Action

For Executive-Level Leaders – Keep your ego out of the decision-making equation. Work to do what's "right" for your business and ignore the "noise" that can come when your colleagues see things differently.

For Mid-Level Leaders – When practicing the development of this habit, be sure to consider how your response (to the question of whether to escalate a conflict) lines up with the vision, goals, and objectives of your organization – this will help you to know whether escalation makes sense.

For Supervisory-Level Leaders – Practice asking this question whenever you deem it necessary. By doing so, you will develop a habit that you can count on as you continue to gain additional responsibilities over the course of your career.

Idea Crosswalk

- **Leadership Mindset** – Tolerance is something a leader can practice and, by which, garner great respect from their employees.
- **Vision** – A more tolerant and patient workplace makes it easier for people to perform at their best, a key element of most strategic visions.
- **People and Talent** – People learn from their leaders, a more open-minded leader leads to more tolerance among staff members.
- **Trust and Empowerment** – We build trust by being more understanding of others.
- **Change Management** – Because change is a challenging subject for most people, being more charitable to others as they embrace change sets a positive tone that leads to greater change acceptance among key stakeholders.

Express your gratitude and share credit, it serves to motivate

Leaders who consistently express gratitude and share credit with their team enhance credibility and effectiveness.

Guru Guidance

Expressing gratitude and acknowledging team members' contributions can boost their morale and motivation. When individuals feel appreciated and recognized for their efforts, they are more likely to be engaged and enthusiastic about their work.

Sharing credit reinforces a sense of teamwork and collaboration. It sends the message that success is a collective effort and that every team member's contributions are valued. This nurtures a stronger sense of unity and cohesion within the team.

> *" ... when leaders give credit where it's due, they build trust ... "*

Moreover, when leaders give credit where it's due, they build trust within their team. Team members are more likely to trust and respect a leader who acknowledges their efforts and doesn't take all the credit for themselves.

So, share the wealth!

After all, expressing gratitude and sharing credit with the team is not only a sign of mature leadership but also a powerful tool for stimulating motivation, trust, and collaboration within the enterprise.

Indeed, expressing gratitude contributes to a positive work culture and leads to long-term business success.

DOI: 10.4324/9781003422754-53

How to Put It into Action

For Executive-Level Leaders – Be accessible. Make yourself available for open communication. Encourage team members to approach you with ideas, concerns, or feedback, and respond in a supportive and appreciative manner.

For Mid-Level Leaders – Lead by example. Show your team how you value and appreciate their work by expressing gratitude and sharing credit with them. Your behavior will set the tone for how those leaders interact with their people.

For Supervisory-Level Leaders – Ask for feedback from your team about your leadership style and whether they feel adequately recognized and appreciated. Use this feedback to refine your approach.

Idea Crosswalk

- **Leadership Mindset** – Top leaders must promote a culture of peer recognition where team members appreciate each other's efforts.
- **Vision** – A captivating vision acknowledges the contribution of every team member, regardless of their role or level within the organization.
- **People and Talent** – Talent is enhanced when, after acknowledging a job well done, leaders discuss what worked and how it can be built upon for future endeavors.
- **Trust and Empowerment** – Trust builds as achievements are celebrated and staffers are recognized for their role in an enterprise's success.
- **Change Management** – The process of change is enriched through publicly recognizing and sharing credit for milestone accomplishments along the way.

Use the *Decency Acid Test* when making a tough, ethical decision

It is a great tool to use if you're in doubt about which way is right.

Guru Guidance

Decent people are more likely to uphold ethical standards and make morally sound decisions. Apply the following whenever confounded by possible ramifications of a pending decision.

At one point in his tenure as Chairman and CEO of Baxter International, Harry Kraemer had to lay off several thousand people. When it was announced, a business reporter asked him how he could sleep at night, to which, Kraemer brilliantly responded:

"I ask myself two questions:

> *" . . . it demonstrates the great care, concern, and empathy* one should consider when approaching tough decisions."

1. *Did I do what I thought was the right thing to do?*
2. *Did I do my best?*

If so, I can sleep.[1]"

What's exceptional about Kraemer's reply is that it demonstrates the great care, concern, and empathy one should consider when approaching tough decisions. Clearly, decency plays a large part in his character.

It inspired me to use these same two questions as something that I fashioned into a *Decency Acid Test.*

If you answer "yes" to both of its questions, you're likely operating decently. If not, it's time to reevaluate your decision.

After all, you want to lead "decently" because leaders care about the well-being of their team members, both personally and professionally – and this leads to improved job satisfaction, reduced stress, and healthier work-life integration for employees.

DOI: 10.4324/9781003422754-54

How to Put It into Action

For Executive-Level Leaders – Practice *feeding forward*! It's a terrific concept to fold into your repertoire. Instead of rehashing all of the things that a team member has done unsatisfactorily, focus on providing advice on what they can do in the future to improve how they operate. After all, we can't change what has happened in the past. However, we can choose to make changes in the future. Feedforward and watch your decency quotient rise across the enterprise.

For Mid-Level Leaders – Show your team of leaders that leadership and common decency are not mutually exclusive ideas. Take the time to reinforce your use of the *Decency Acid Test* by explaining how you arrived at tough, ethical decisions. The more that you do, the more your leaders will follow suit.

For Supervisory-Level Leaders – Bringing common decency back to business requires that we actually begin to live, and behave, by the *Golden Rule*. So, in all of your interactions with your team, "Do unto them, as you would have them do unto you."

Idea Crosswalk

- **Leadership Mindset** – Leaders who consistently act decently earn the trust and respect of their team members and peers.
- **Vision** – Decency should be a cornerstone of every strategic vision.
- **People and Talent** – A strong reputation by using the *Decency Acid Test* can attract top talent, customers, and partners, contributing to the long-term success of the enterprise.
- **Trust and Empowerment** – Decency creates a stable and positive work environment that supports growth and builds trust among the workforce.
- **Change Management** – Decency promotes effective problem-solving and conflict resolution during times of change.

Note

1   *The Indispensable Conversation Podcast*, hosted by James M. Kerr, November 15, 2021. https://podcasters.spotify.com/pod/show/indispensableconversation/episodes/Harry-Kraemer--Jr----Should-We-Care-About-Decency-in-Leadership-Within-corporate-America-e1aajvq/a-a6tel86

Outstanding leaders "own" it!

Taking responsibility for the good and the bad improves an organization's culture by encouraging honesty, openness, and shared accountability.

Guru Guidance

When leaders "own" both successes and failures, it instills confidence in staffers and customers, alike. They appreciate leaders who are forthright about challenges and responsive to feedback, which enhances an organization's brand value in the marketplace.

Exceptional leaders understand the importance of accountability. They recognize that accountability is a fundamental aspect of leadership and that they must take responsibility for the outcomes and performance of their teams and the organization as a whole.

> *"By owning both the good and the bad, the most respected leaders set a powerful example for their teams to follow."*

Additionally, outstanding leaders lead by example. They understand that if they want their team members to take ownership of their actions and responsibilities, they must demonstrate that quality themselves. By owning both the good and the bad, the most respected leaders set a powerful example for their teams to follow.

Also, strong leadership "ownership" demonstrates integrity and transparency. Extraordinary leaders are honest about their organization's successes and challenges. They communicate openly with their teams, stakeholders, and customers, and seek to build trust and credibility along the way.

In fact, when leaders take responsibility when things don't go as planned, they boost customer loyalty, too. By not deflecting blame or shifting responsibility they demonstrate a commitment to actively work to find solutions and make decisions that improve customer trust in the enterprise.

DOI: 10.4324/9781003422754-55

Indeed, outstanding leaders "own" the good and the bad because they exemplify accountability, set a positive example, demonstrate integrity and transparency, and build trust with stakeholders – positioning the organization for continued success.

How to Put It into Action

For Executive-Level Leaders – Hold yourself accountable for your performance and the performance of your organization. This means acknowledging and addressing shortcomings or failures and taking corrective actions as needed.

For Mid-Level Leaders – When challenges arise within your area of responsibility, actively engage with your team in problem-solving and decision-making to address them.

For Supervisory-Level Leaders – Accept responsibility for your decisions, actions, and the outcomes that result from them.

Idea Crosswalk

- **Leadership Mindset** – Leaders who exhibit their accountability for outcomes encourage a mentality of continuous improvement among staffers.
- **Vision** – A leadership team that takes full responsibility for successes and failures ensures that their actions are aligned with the organization's vision. This alignment is essential for maintaining a clear and consistent focus on long-term objectives.
- **People and Talent** – Open and honest communication about an organization's performance, both positive and negative, improves morale.
- **Trust and Empowerment** – Leaders who "own" both sides of the performance equation are seen as trustworthy.
- **Change Management** – To successfully drive change within an enterprise requires leaders to take ownership of their actions and decisions along the way.

Part IV

People and Talent Tips

Indispensable leaders understand how to get the best from their people. They understand their team members' strengths aligning tasks and responsibilities with individual capabilities. They create an inclusive environment that values different perspectives, experiences, and strengths, leading to a more innovative and high-performing organization.

The best leaders enable people to perform better. They identify their people's areas for improvement, too. They provide constructive feedback and offer opportunities for learning and growth so to enhance their organization's ability to outperform the competition.

The most skillful leaders understand that business is a team sport. They empower their people by trusting them with responsibilities and decision-making. This demonstrates confidence in their team's abilities and encourages autonomy and ownership among team members.

These tips are intended to help leaders to lead their team while developing the talent required for enduring success.

DOI: 10.4324/9781003422754-56

Leadership Tip 52

Surround yourself with people who make you better

Working with individuals who have different viewpoints can help you see problems from multiple angles and develop more well-rounded solutions.

Guru Guidance

Establish an open and safe environment for your people to express themselves. Ask for reaction and feedback on your ideas. Actively listen to their response. Show genuine interest and ideas that make sense, and you will forge a team that will give you what you need to hear.

To be sure, leaders who surround themselves with people who challenge them are less likely to make hasty or biased decisions. Engaging with those who make us think through our initial perceptions can lead to more well-informed and balanced decision-making.

> *" . . . thought-provokingcollaborators can help you refine your leadership style and values."*

Further, thought-provoking collaborators can help you refine your leadership style and values. Over time, you'll develop a more authentic leadership approach that reflects your core values and principles. These people make you better.

Also, seeking additional opinions from colleagues can inspire innovation and creativity because it introduces new ideas, techniques, or strategies that you may not have ordinarily considered otherwise.

Of course, working with individuals who challenge you can lead to conflicts and disagreements. However, these conflicts provide an opportunity to hone your conflict resolution skills. In the long run, this can be tremendously beneficial to you and them.

Indeed, collaborating with people from whom you can learn fosters personal and professional growth, improves your leadership abilities, and leads to better decision-making – all characteristics that ultimately make you more effective.

DOI: 10.4324/9781003422754-57

How to Put It into Action

For Executive-Level Leaders – Avoid dismissing ideas outright, even if they seem unconventional. Instead, take those opportunities to practice humility. Being more open to, and examining, a wider range of alternatives is often the path to better solutions.

For Mid-Level Leaders – When problem-solving, offer an initial solution then ask your team to pick it apart. Try to understand the reasons behind their challenges and objections. Extend the thinking by reacting to and/or incorporating some of the ideas offered.

For Supervisory-Level Leaders – When receiving feedback from your leader, avoid reacting emotionally or defensively. Consider, instead, that there could be some fresh thinking offered that might be worth incorporating into your go-forward approach.

Idea Crosswalk

- **Leadership Mindset** – The most inspiring leaders encourage feedback and constructive criticism.
- **Vision** – Patience is a virtue, and it is a crucial part of enabling a workplace that accepts and encourages differing points of view. These are characteristics that should be discussed in an organization's vision story.
- **Company Culture** – As leaders approach collaboration with a genuine willingness to learn and grow, they strengthen the company culture.
- **Trust and Empowerment** – Demonstrating empathy when listening and responding to objections from team members helps to build a workplace based on trust.
- **Change Management** – It is a leader's responsibility to establish the common ground required to make change happen within the organization.

There is no such thing as too much communication!

Frequent communication helps keep everyone aligned and moving in the same direction.

Guru Guidance

Be transparent in your communication. Share information about the organization's goals, challenges, and decisions. Keep team members informed to the greatest extent possible to keep them committed to the cause.

> *"When people feel informed and involved, they are more likely to be motivated and committed to their work and the organization's mission."*

When leaders communicate extensively, it helps to ensure that everyone understands what is expected of them. Clear and frequent communication is fundamental to conveying a leader's vision, goals, and expectations to the enterprise.

In today's day and age, leaders need to adapt and pivot as circumstances change. Effective communication helps staffers stay better informed and enables them to adapt their work and priorities accordingly.

During times of crises, for example, leaders who communicate regularly and transparently can help calm fears, provide guidance, and maintain a sense of stability and direction.

In addition, it builds trust. Leaders who communicate openly will earn the trust of their people. It also enhances the likelihood of receiving valuable feedback from staffers, as they come to realize that delivering "bad news" will not be held against them.

Further, communication can serve as an accelerant of engagement. By sharing successes, recognizing achievements, and expressing gratitude, leaders can boost morale and motivation among team members. When

DOI: 10.4324/9781003422754-58

people feel informed and involved, they become more committed to their work and the organization's mission.

How to Put It into Action

For Executive-Level Leaders – Communication is your job! Don't let people guess what you want or what is happening within the organization. Communicate important information early and often.

For Mid-Level Leaders – Commit to scheduling and conducting regular team meetings, including both one-on-one check-ins and group meetings, to provide updates, share information, and address questions and concerns. Consistency is a key to success, so maintain a regular schedule for these updates.

For Supervisory-Level Leaders – Utilize various communication channels such as email, meetings, video conferencing, instant messaging, and other collaborative platforms to reach different team members.

Idea Crosswalk

- **Leadership Mindset** – Leaders can "up" their communications game by fostering an environment where team members feel comfortable asking questions and providing input.
- **Vision** – Frequent communication helps keep everyone aligned and moving toward the achievement of the strategic vision of the enterprise.
- **Company Culture** – Effective communication allows leaders to share knowledge and insights, promote continuous learning, and support the development of team members – reinforcing a winning culture.
- **Trust and Empowerment** – Active and consistent communication is a cornerstone of building trust, alignment, engagement, and successful teamwork within an organization.
- **Change Management** – The use of tools that facilitate seamless communication across an organization improves the outcomes of change initiatives.

Learn to tell your story so others want to hear more

All great stories follow a certain form. Your story can and should be used to build connection.

Guru Guidance

Telling your story is a powerful tool for engaging and inspiring others. By sharing your personal journey, you become more relatable and, when done in an inspiring way, it serves as a wonderful motivator for your staffers.

Sharing one's origin story demonstrates vulnerability and authenticity. When leaders open up about their personal experiences, it helps build trust within the organization. People are more likely to trust and connect with someone who is willing to share their own challenges and successes.

> " . . . *everyone has a story, and when a leader shares their own, it humanizes them.*"

Also, everyone has a story, and when a leader shares their own, it humanizes them. It shows that they, too, have faced obstacles, made mistakes, and overcome challenges. This makes the leader seem approachable and relatable, encouraging others in the organization to open up and connect with colleagues on a deeper level, too.

Indeed, when a leader shares their story it helps people to believe that they, too, can overcome obstacles and achieve their goals.

Here's a simple formula to use to help you develop your origin story:

1. **Start Strong:** Every story needs a strong start. Be sure to begin yours with something that can grab attention and pull people in.
2. **Introduce Your Antagonist:** All "heroes" must overcome some challenge that stands between them and their goal.
3. **Highlight A Trusted Advisor:** We all have guides that befriend us all along the way. Be sure to mention them.

DOI: 10.4324/9781003422754-59

4. **Sprinkle In Some Magic:** It's that special something you did to overcome the antagonist.
5. **Bring It Home:** A great story needs an ending that ties it all together. Make yours snap!

I use this with my coaching clients all the time. So, I know it works!

How to Put It into Action

For **Executive-Level Leaders** – Use the formula to develop your story. Tell it at your next company-wide meeting to complement other information that you want to convey at that time.

For **Mid-Level Leaders** – Yes, your story is worth telling. Use the method offered here to develop your story and share it with your team of leaders.

For **Supervisory-Level Leaders** – You can inspire your people when they need it by telling them your story. Use the technique outlined to craft the one you want to share.

Idea Crosswalk

- **Leadership Mindset** – Origin stories contain valuable life lessons. By sharing their own experiences, leaders impart wisdom to their people.
- **Vision** – By sharing their journey, leaders can emphasize the importance of their vision and the difference the achievement of that vision will make for the entire enterprise.
- **Company Culture** – Storytelling is a powerful tool for evoking emotions. When leaders share their origin story, they create an emotional connection that can influence company culture.
- **Trust and Empowerment** – Sharing an origin story is just the beginning. It can pique interest and make people curious about what comes next. This curiosity leads to increased trust and engagement.
- **Change Management** – A leader's story can be used as a tool for motivating others to want to be a part of the change the leader is spearheading.

Show up, your team deserves your full attention

It demonstrates that you value their efforts and are willing to roll up your sleeves, too.

Guru Guidance

Being present allows leaders to build strong and meaningful relationships with their team members. This, in turn, fosters trust, mutual respect, and a sense of belonging. It leads to a more cohesive and collaborative work environment, as well.

Being absorbed in the work activities of your team demonstrates your commitment to their success. It allows you to provide real-time support and guidance as needed. If team members encounter obstacles, have questions, or need assistance, your presence and engagement will make problem-solving more efficient.

> *"All things equal, your presence should serve as a motivational factor for your team."*

Undoubtedly, complex issues and challenges arise throughout the workday. Your active engagement allows you to identify and address problems as they occur, preventing them from escalating into larger issues that hinder long-term progress.

On the other hand, leaders must avoid becoming overbearing. Team members are more likely to approach you with their ideas and feedback when they perceive you as a resource, and not someone there to simply direct their every move.

All things equal, your presence should serve as a motivational factor for your team. When they see you actively involved and invested in their work, it inspires a sense of shared purpose and accountability. Team members take their tasks more seriously when they know their leader is engaged.

DOI: 10.4324/9781003422754-60

How to Put It into Action

For **Executive-Level Leaders** – Establish clear expectations for leaders regarding their presence, participation, and engagement within their teams.

For **Mid-Level Leaders** – Routinely engage with your team during work activities. It fosters stronger relationships and trust.

For **Supervisory-Level Leaders** – Participate in the work. You will gain valuable insights into the challenges and intricacies of the work by being involved in it. This firsthand knowledge will help you to better support your team in the future, too.

Idea Crosswalk

- **Leadership Mindset** – Leaders who are fully engaged in their team's work activities provide immediate support and build strong working relationships. These relationships, ultimately, contribute to the overall success of the organization.
- **Vision** – A vision that describes a work setting that holds leaders accountable for their presence and engagement with their teams tends to inspire people to bring their best effort to their jobs each day.
- **Company Culture** – By promoting an environment where leaders are approachable and accessible, organizations foster a culture that values leadership presence.
- **Trust and Empowerment** – Strong leadership presence in the workplace builds trust.
- **Change Management** – By insisting that senior leaders be involved in change activities, organizations showcase the importance of active leadership engagement.

Before pointing your finger, use your thumb!

Being accountable for what you say and do is a crucial part of any leader's job.

Guru Guidance

Acknowledge any mistakes that you make openly and honestly. Avoid creating excuses, downplaying the error, or blaming others. Take ownership of what you do.

It can't be stressed enough: leaders must "own" their actions and never shift blame to their peers or underlings.

After all, integrity is a fundamental aspect of effective leadership. Leaders who blame others before examining their own actions can appear hypocritical and lacking in integrity. This erodes trust and minimizes their effectiveness – no one goes above and beyond for someone whom they don't respect.

> " . . . leaders who are accountable for their words and actions earn the admiration of their people."

On the other hand, leaders who are accountable for their words and actions earn the admiration of their people.

With that, it's important to note that this does not mean leaders should always assume blame for every situation, either. Rather, leaders should be willing to examine their actions and decisions objectively and take responsibility as appropriate.

How to Put It into Action

For Executive-Level Leaders – Never make excuses for poor performance. Instead, take full responsibility for it and show your people that "*the buck stops here*" with you.

For Mid-Level Leaders – Accept your share of the responsibility in situations where conflicts arise. This will better equip you to facilitate

DOI: 10.4324/9781003422754-61

constructive discussions and find resolutions while rousing the trust of your team of leaders.

For Supervisory-Level Leaders – Taking responsibility for your actions demonstrates empathy and understanding towards your team members who may also make mistakes. An empathetic leadership approach will lead to stronger work relationships and a more supportive business environment.

Idea Crosswalk

- **Leadership Mindset** – The most respected leaders have adopted a philosophy of taking responsibility for their actions and decisions before shifting any responsibility to others.
- **Vision** – A robust vision story describes work settings where people take responsibility for their actions and demonstrate empathy and understanding towards team members who may also make mistakes.
- **Company Culture** – When leaders take responsibility for their actions, it sets an obvious example for their team members and establishes a culture of accountability within the organization.
- **Trust and Empowerment** – When staffers see their leaders accepting blame and acknowledging mistakes, it provides an opportunity for them to learn and grow as individuals and professionals, as well – reinforcing trust along the way.
- **Change Management** – Blaming others during change activities can create a toxic work environment, where team members fear being scapegoated. On the other hand, when leaders accept fault when appropriate, team members feel safe to voice concerns, share ideas, and admit their own mistakes. This improves the ways in which change is implemented.

Patience is a decision you get to make

Patience is an important part of leading others because driving change takes time.

Guru Guidance

When impatience seems to be rearing its ugly head, it could be time to remember that you can choose to be patient, instead.

As top business leaders, we can, and should, strive to act with graciousness, dignity, and a strong sense of propriety at all times. If we want to be the kind of leaders that warrant respect and admiration, we must have patience with others, and ourselves.

> *" . . . the opposite of patience is not impatience. Rather, the opposite of patience is anxiousness."*

Of course, we can choose to fly off the handle, point fingers, and resort to a whole range of other bad behaviors in a fruitless effort to feel less anxious about things not happening at the pace and in the ways in which we wished they would. But that kind of behavior is not likely to make things better. Exhibiting some patience might improve the situation.

Indeed, the opposite of patience is not impatience. Rather, the opposite of patience is anxiousness.

We begin to feel anxious when things seem slow or to be heading in the wrong direction. We become anxious at the thought of losing time, wasting cycles on waiting and seeing, and, not optimizing the way we are leading others and ourselves.

However, the reality is we do not control the universe. In fact, the only thing that we can hope to ever control is ourselves. So, choose to be patient. It shows others that you have what it takes to face tough challenges.

DOI: 10.4324/9781003422754-62

How to Put It into Action

For Executive-Level Leaders – The best way to regulate your behavior as a top leader is to slow down long enough and give what you're feeling a name. This requires that you stay in the moment and not over-amplify the consequences of whatever it is that is making you feel impatient. By naming the feeling, you give yourself the time to gain insight into what's really going on inside – and you're practicing patience by doing so.

For Mid-Level Leaders – Before blowing your top the next time your team of leaders fails to live up to your expectations, try this: remind yourself that most people are decent and are trying their best. This helps you to choose a more patient way to react. Try it. It works!

For Supervisory-Level Leaders – The more prepared your team is to succeed, the less likely you will need to exercise patience with them. Why? Because a better-prepared team accomplishes more good things, faster than a team that lacks fundamental competence. Commit to developing your team and you will almost automatically become more patient.

Idea Crosswalk

- **Leadership Mindset** – Leaders should encourage staffers to be patient with one another.
- **Vision** – Winning vision stories characterize patience as an advantage to be gained over competitors that rush in and make mistakes.
- **Company Culture** – A work environment that emphasizes the notion that patience is a choice enables a calmer culture to emerge.
- **Trust and Empowerment** – Trust is built when leaders choose to be patient with themselves and others in the workplace.
- **Change Management** – Change initiatives take time and perseverance. Patience is required to see the most challenging change efforts through to fruition.

Going flatter only works when your team is properly prepared

Flatter organizations are often better equipped to adapt to rapidly changing business situations and swiftly shifting market conditions.

Guru Guidance

A flatter organization structure only works when staff are prepared and equipped to self-manage – escalating issues only when it is out of their decision rights to make the call. Commit to developing and preparing your people so they can "run flat."

There are fewer layers of management between the top executives and front-line employees in flatter organizations. This can lead to quicker and more agile decision-making since there are fewer approval processes and less bureaucracy to navigate.

> *"This leads to improved responsiveness and an enhanced customer experience."*

Further, it allows for more direct top-to-frontline communication and problem-solving. Because there are fewer managerial positions in the operation it lowers administrative costs, too.

But that's not all! A more customer-centric business operation results because "flatter" means decision-making is driven closer to the customer-facing parts of the business – leading to improved responsiveness and an enhanced customer experience.

Of course, for any of this to work, staffers must be properly trained and prepared to make appropriate decisions as needed. If they're not adequately prepared to self-manage, the organization is sure to suffer the consequences.

To sum up, the choice of organizational structure should align with the company's goals, size, industry, and specific needs. Balancing the advantages of flatter reporting lines with the potential drawbacks, such as the need for more personnel training, stronger automation, and the right

DOI: 10.4324/9781003422754-63

kind of leadership mindset (more interested in empowering than directing employees), is crucial for achieving the right organizational fit.

How to Put It into Action

For Executive-Level Leaders – Understand the existing organizational culture and assess whether a flatter structure is needed to meet the goals of the enterprise. If so, direct your people to make it happen.

For Mid-Level Leaders – Evaluate the current organizational structure, identifying areas that can be streamlined or eliminated. Create teams to explore options to flatten the reporting lines.

For Supervisory-Level Leaders – Assess if employees at all levels have the necessary skills and competencies to thrive in a flatter organization. Offer training and development programs as needed.

Idea Crosswalk

- **Leadership Mindset** – Leaders need to streamline decision-making processes to ensure efficiency and responsiveness.
- **Vision** – A strategic vision for a company aiming to adopt a flatter reporting structure should articulate the overarching goals, guiding principles, and key elements of the transformation envisioned.
- **Company Culture** – Company cultures change when leaders strive to run flatter through the formation of self-managed, cross-functional teams.
- **Trust and Empowerment** – Leaders must trust and develop their teams to go flat while encouraging and empowering employees to take the initiative and be more autonomous in their decision-making.
- **Change Management** – Leaders must implement comprehensive change management strategies to guide the organization through the transition and be prepared to proactively address staffer resistance.

"Customer first" works, once you take care of your staff

Engaged employees are emotionally invested in their work, which translates into higher job satisfaction and a willingness to go the extra mile for the customer.

Guru Guidance

Make the psychological safety of your team members a top priority. Create a work setting that centers on their development and care so they can attend to your customer's needs.

The workplace can be a significant source of stress for staffers. Leaders can create a healthier, more sustainable work environment by promoting work-life integration and employee well-being.

> *" . . . there is a direct link between employee satisfaction and customer satisfaction."*

Indeed, ensuring the welfare of employees is a fundamental moral and ethical responsibility. It demonstrates empathy and compassion for the people who contribute to the organization's success. Happy and healthy staff members are more engaged, productive, and loyal.

Further, there is a direct link between employee satisfaction and customer satisfaction. Contented employees tend to provide better customer service, resulting in higher customer loyalty and greater brand value.

In fact, when leaders prioritize their staff's well-being, they can expect increased productivity, higher quality work, and a greater commitment to the goals of the enterprise. Not to mention, showing care for employees is a key factor in retaining them, too.

DOI: 10.4324/9781003422754-64

How to Put It into Action

For Executive-Level Leaders – Promote mental health awareness and offer resources for employees to manage stress, anxiety, and work-related pressures.

For Mid-Level Leaders – Implement wellness initiatives that support your people's physical health. You can do this by providing fitness programs, health screenings, and access to nutritious food options in company facilities.

For Supervisory-Level Leaders – When appropriate, provide flexible work arrangements, such as remote work options or flexible scheduling, to accommodate your team's personal needs.

Idea Crosswalk

- **Leadership Mindset** – A leader's care for their staff translates into better support of the customer because happy people deliver impeccable customer experiences.
- **Vision** – Leaders who support their people must be weaved into the vision for the enterprise.
- **Company Culture** – A culture that prioritizes employee well-being and support contributes to a positive work environment – one that takes care of its customers.
- **Trust and Empowerment** – Caring for employees is not only good for business; it also helps to build trust among staffers.
- **Change Management** – During major change implementation, leaders need the training necessary to support and manage their teams effectively, including handling employee well-being issues.

Even world-class athletes have coaches!

Welcome those who can teach you new things, they will make you better.

Guru Guidance

If you believe leadership training alone is enough to build the community of leaders required to stay ahead of the competition, think again! Personalized leadership coaching is the best way to help your leaders become exceptional.

Coaches simply help people to perform at their best.

That's why most world-class athletes all have coaches. Their performance is optimized through good coaching. Why not secure coaching for you and your community of leaders? They deserve exceptional coaching, too. It will make them better in so many ways, including:

- Enriched Relationships
- Better Decision-Making
- Enhanced Management Skills
- Greater Presence
- Stronger "Followership"
- Increased Preparedness
- Less Stress
- Exceptional Business Performance
- More Positive Self-Talk

> *"The 'right' coach delivers the tough stuff!"*

But, you must be sure to choose a coach that can give you what you need. The "right" coach delivers the tough stuff!

Indeed, the "right" coach must be courageous enough to tell their client something they may not want to hear. Of course, many coaches avoid doing this. After all, it stirs conflict. It's uncomfortable. It's risky to the coach's business (what if the client can't handle the message and decides to fire the coach?).

DOI: 10.4324/9781003422754-65

Find a qualified person who possesses the skills, experience, and fearlessness to make you and your team better and you will see your results improve.

How to Put It into Action

For Executive-Level Leaders – Look for coaches who specialize in leadership development. Consider factors such as their experience, coaching approach, and client testimonials.

For Mid-Level Leaders – Work with the selected coach to create a customized coaching plan that outlines the specific focus areas, timelines, and the number of coaching sessions required.

For Supervisory-Level Leaders – When being coached, provide feedback to the coach about their effectiveness, and discuss any adjustments or changes needed in their coaching process that could make their effort more effective for you.

Idea Crosswalk

- **Leadership Mindset** – Leadership coaching is an ongoing process that, when fully embraced, will improve leadership effectiveness within the enterprise.
- **Vision** – A vision that encourages leaders to share their coaching experiences and insights with each other enables peer learning and leads to the creation of a supportive community of leaders.
- **Company Culture** – Coaching helps leaders enhance their skills, foster a collaborative work setting, and ultimately drive positive change within the organization.
- **Trust and Empowerment** – Any areas for improvement a leader may have related to trust-building and empowerment can be bettered through one-on-one coaching sessions.
- **Change Management** – Coaches are valuable in helping leaders manage change.

Being "in it together" is a boundless multiplier

The best teams are staffed by people who believe that they can trust and depend on each other to get the job done.

Guru Guidance

Be flexible and adaptable to changes and challenges. Lead the team through transitions by demonstrating resilience and a willingness to adapt to evolving circumstances.

> *" . . . a leader's selflessness will have a positive impact on team morale."*

When leaders prioritize the company's overall success over personal interests, it increases the likelihood of achieving the organization's goals and objectives. This focus contributes to the company's growth and competitiveness while providing the inspiration needed to propel staffers to greater heights of performance.

Indeed, a leader's selfless behavior has a positive impact on a team's morale. It fosters a sense of unity and shared purpose among employees and leads to a more motivated and productive workforce.

Likewise, putting aside parochial interests encourages collaboration and teamwork among departments. When leaders work together for the benefit of the enterprise, it leads to more effective problem-solving and greater innovation, which translates into superior business results in the marketplace.

Certainly, a company with a strong, values-driven leadership approach is attractive to prospective employees, too. Stated simply, employees are more likely to stay in an organization whose leaders put the goals of the company ahead of their own personal goals. This builds loyalty and solidarity within the workforce.

DOI: 10.4324/9781003422754-66

How to Put It into Action

For Executive-Level Leaders – Whenever possible, encourage the creation of a culture where parochial interests are set aside and inspire the free flow of ideas for the good of the company.

For Mid-Level Leaders – Encourage and facilitate collaboration within your team of leaders and across departments. Recognize and reward teamwork and cross-functional cooperation.

For Supervisory-Level Leaders – Work to set a positive example that promotes teamwork. It demonstrates that putting personal agendas aside leads to positive outcomes for everyone.

Idea Crosswalk

- **Leadership Mindset** – Leaders, who put the "company good," ahead of their own advancement, are more likely to build organizations that are better equipped to adapt to changing market conditions, technological advancements, and customer needs.
- **Vision** – A vision story should describe a leadership team that is committed to the company's long-term success and profitability.
- **Company Culture** – An extraordinary culture is one where employees are aligned with the company's goals, and work with an "all for one, one for all" mindset.
- **Trust and Empowerment** – Leaders who behave in ways that demonstrate selflessness for the good of the company build trust and credibility with employees and customers, alike.
- **Change Management** – Change teams work best when they collaborate, share knowledge, and innovate for the good of the enterprise.

Sometimes you will need to coach

Regardless of how talented and motivated the team is, they will often need you to teach and coach them on how to get the job done in the best ways possible.

Guru Guidance

When coaching your people, encourage each person to reflect on what they're learning and what they want to continue to improve on in the future. Help them set new goals and practice new leadership skills as they move forward. This helps your coaching stick!

Coaching helps to motivate and engage team members. When leaders invest time and effort in coaching their people, staffers feel valued and inspired. Furthermore, retention and loyalty improve, too. Most people are likely to stay with an organization that invests in their personal and professional growth.

> " . . . staffers feel valued and inspired."

Additionally, coaching enables leaders to help team members address challenges and overcome obstacles. Done right, coaching encourages open and honest dialogue, which can lead to stronger working relationships across the enterprise.

Once a coaching paradigm becomes an established element of leadership development within an enterprise, it prompts other leaders to use coaching as a means of developing their teams, too. In time, most leaders will be coaching their people to help maximize their staffer's skills and capabilities.

With that, team member confidence grows – as "coached up" individuals come to believe in their own abilities to learn new ways to get the job done.

DOI: 10.4324/9781003422754-67

How to Put It into Action

For Executive-Level Leaders – Coaching can be used as a tool for resolving conflicts or addressing interpersonal issues within your team of top leaders. Adopt a coaching mindset to guide team members toward better collaboration and communication.

For Mid-Level Leaders – Use coaching to reinforce and align your team of leaders with the organization's culture, values, and mission, creating a more cohesive and united community of next-level leaders.

For Supervisory-Level Leaders – Start coaching your people! It provides opportunities to develop your own leadership skills. Through mentoring and guiding others, you will gain valuable experience and insights into how to be more effective, as well.

Idea Crosswalk

- **Leadership Mindset** – Leaders who invest in the development of their team members create a positive impact that endures even after they've moved on to new roles or organizations.
- **Vision** – Coaching can serve as the bridge from vision to practice.
- **Company Culture** – Coaching is instrumental in grooming future leaders within the organization, ensuring that the culture continues to flourish.
- **Trust and Empowerment** – Coaching inspires open and honest communication, which builds stronger working relationships and trust.
- **Change Management** – By providing feedback and personalized guidance through coaching, leaders can smooth the path for the change process.

Leadership Tip 63

Winning teams require connection

Connection underpins true collaboration, trust, and shared inspiration.

Guru Guidance

Promote continuous learning within your organization. Encourage members to share their knowledge and experiences with one another, creating a culture of learning – it builds connection that lasts.

Building and nurturing solid connections among team members is a vital aspect of effective teamwork. A strong relationship among teammates enhances a team's ability to perform at its best, overcome challenges, and achieve desired results.

> *Team members who feel connected never want to do anything that will let their teammates down ... "*

Work teams that possess rock-solid member connections are better equipped to adapt to changes and other unforeseen circumstances that crop up in the course of doing business. Good interpersonal relationships enable colleagues to make needed adjustments more seamlessly.

Collaboration among these kinds of teams is just better! We all know that collaboration is essential for overcoming complex challenges and overall better performance.

The same can be said for trust. When team members trust each other they communicate openly, rely on each person to do their job, and work together to achieve success.

The simple fact is team members who feel a deep connection with each other never want to do anything that will let their teammates down or threaten the success of the team. This goes a long way towards motivating people to give their all to the effort.

Indeed, when individuals know that their teammates have their back, they go above and beyond to perform at their highest level.

DOI: 10.4324/9781003422754-68

How to Put It into Action

For Executive-Level Leaders – Help to build strong connections among staffers by encouraging your direct reports to provide guidance and support to newer or less-experienced employees.

For Mid-Level Leaders – Encourage cross-functional collaboration in order to build needed relationships among people from different areas of the enterprise.

For Supervisory-Level Leaders – Embolden team members to resolve issues collaboratively, and provide guidance when necessary. This helps build personal connections among teammates.

Idea Crosswalk

- **Leadership Mindset** – Transparency contributes to connection-building among leaders and a shared sense of ownership in the outcomes of those decisions among staffers.
- **Vision** – Teamwork, characterized by deep relationships among staffers, is always an element of any compelling vision.
- **Company Culture** – Strong connections among employees make a culture more resilient. When setbacks or challenges arise, teams with a strong sense of connection are better equipped to weather adversity, bounce back, and continue working toward their goals.
- **Trust and Empowerment** – When team members share solid relationships, they trust each other. Greater trust ensures that everyone is pulling in the same direction.
- **Change Management** – Positive relationships, shared victories, and a supportive atmosphere contribute to a sense of fulfillment and well-being among team members, which always leads to better performance in change efforts.

If two people are in constant agreement, you probably only need one of them!

The notion highlights the importance of diversity of thought and perspectives in collaborative and decision-making processes.

Guru Guidance

We want staffers to think for themselves. Celebrate instances where team members take the initiative and think outside the box. Recognize and appreciate their independent thinking done in the spirit of making a difference to the enterprise.

While agreement is important in many situations, it should not come at the cost of stifling creativity, innovation, or critical thinking.

Indeed, differing viewpoints and healthy disagreements can lead to better outcomes because they force individuals to consider alternative perspectives and potential flaws in one's own ideas. With that, when two people constantly agree with each other, it may indicate a lack of critical thinking capabilities or an unhealthy dependence. Neither are good for business!

> *" . . . when two people constantly agree with each other, it may indicate a lack of critical thinking capabilities . . . "*

Keep in mind that breakthrough thinking only arises from the clash of differing opinions and approaches. When individuals with varying viewpoints collaborate, they can generate creative solutions and new ideas that might not have emerged if they simply agreed all the time.

Further, constant agreement may lead to one-sided, biased decisions. Having multiple perspectives ensures a more balanced and well-considered approach to problem-solving and strategy development. Leaders must cultivate this among their staffers.

DOI: 10.4324/9781003422754-69

How to Put It into Action

For Executive-Level Leaders – Set the tone by consistently emphasizing the value of sharing diverse perspectives. Encourage your people to speak truth to power.

For Mid-Level Leaders – Encourage your people to think for themselves. Ensure that decision-making processes involve a range of ideas by prompting your group of leaders for their personal perspectives on the issues being considered.

For Supervisory-Level Leaders – Assemble our team to tackle complex challenges within the group. Solicit viewpoints from each member. Use this interaction as an opportunity to remind them of the importance of cultivating their own solutions to address key issues.

Idea Crosswalk

- **Leadership Mindset** – Having multiple perspectives ensures a more balanced and well-considered approach to problem-solving and strategy development.
- **Vision** – Your vision story should celebrate free and independent thinking.
- **Company Culture** – Encouraging and valuing diverse opinions fosters an inclusive and engaging culture – one where team members feel that their ideas and perspectives are genuinely considered and respected even when they run counter to the prevailing wisdom within the organization.
- **Trust and Empowerment** – Welcoming diverse viewpoints helps enterprises identify ethical issues that might not be immediately evident, otherwise. Circumnavigating these kinds of issues improves the trust quotient within, and outside of, the organization.
- **Change Management** – Creating a work setting that welcomes differing perspectives helps to identify potential threats and opportunities, facilitating more adaptive change responses to the issues uncovered.

Resiliency-building is a multi-faceted proposition

One's mind, body, spirit, and community must be "right" to be truly resilient during the most challenging of times.

Guru Guidance

Conduct regular one-on-one meetings with team members to discuss their well-being, challenges, and resiliency strategies. Provide guidance and support as needed.

There are four aspects of resiliency that require development within each person on your team. These include:

> *" . . . we need to feel mentally, physically, emotionally and socially aligned to feel our best . . . "*

- The **mental** aspect, which helps develop self-regulation skills, and assists people with re-framing thoughts, managing change, and self-awareness.
- The **physical** aspect, which promotes proper sleep, nutrition, and exercise to remain as physically fit as possible.
- The **community** aspect, which emphasizes relationship-building, team-member connection, and social interaction.
- The **"feeding the spirit"** aspect, which is about finding meaning in one's work and workplace.

The integration of these makes a person whole. Indeed, we need to feel mentally, physically, emotionally, and socially aligned to feel our best – confident that we can handle whatever comes our way.

How to Put It into Action

For Executive-Level Leaders – Put a robust resilience program in place and ensure that it's offered regularly.

DOI: 10.4324/9781003422754-70

For **Mid-Level Leaders** – Emphasize that resiliency is a lifelong skill. Encourage your team members to view challenges as opportunities to grow and build a toolkit for resilience that they can carry with them throughout their careers.

For **Supervisory-Level Leaders** – Encourage your people to practice all four parts of personal resiliency. Reinforce these practices and show them that you care about their well-being.

Idea Crosswalk

- **Leadership Mindset** – Leaders should ensure that their employees have access to resources for mental health support, counseling, and assistance programs when needed.
- **Vision** – Resilience enables an organization to adapt, recover, and thrive despite adversity. It should be reflected in a firm's vision story.
- **Company Culture** – A workplace culture that values resilience encourages employees to embrace change, take calculated risks, and learn from failures.
- **Trust and Empowerment** – You can build trust by providing staff with the support and resources that they need to cope with stress and maintain their productivity.
- **Change Management** – An organization can improve strategic outcomes by promoting self-care practices, including exercise, mindfulness, and stress-reduction techniques during all major change activities.

Use silence as a tool

Just because "they" asked, doesn't mean that you have to answer.

Guru Guidance

Take time for personal reflection in silence. This can help you process complex issues, gain clarity, and make well-informed decisions. It's especially useful during times when you're feeling intense pressure to perform at a high level.

Every day, most of us are barraged with questions and issues. They come from every direction, and few can be anticipated. As a consequence, many leaders become extremely reactionary – feeling obliged to immediately answer every question and address every issue that comes their way.

> *" . . . sometimes a request doesn't deserve a response."*

Stop doing that! It's not your duty to respond to every inquiry.

In fact, sometimes a request doesn't deserve a response. Thus, by not responding to some requests, you are sending a message. Just be sure that your use of silence is used deliberately, and you'll be on your way to using it as a tool to manage your messaging.

Further, work to surround yourself with the best possible and competent team to help you address what needs to be done. If you institute appropriate problem escalation and triage practices within that team, you will enable a healthy means to respond to issues and challenges in the most expedient ways.

Keep in mind that you're not always going to have the answers, nor can every question be answered. So, leverage the skills and experiences of your team to harvest the best responses. You will help them to become better leaders and they will help you to better manage the onslaught of challenges that come your way each day.

DOI: 10.4324/9781003422754-71

Of course, it's important to note that using silence as a tool requires a delicate balance. Too much silence can be perceived as indifference or aloofness, while too little can lead to missed opportunities for reflection and understanding. Effective leadership involves knowing when and how to employ silence for maximum impact in different situations.

How to Put It into Action

For Executive-Level Leaders – As a top leader you already know that you don't have to solve every problem. Create the space for your leaders to step up and address issues as they arise.

For Mid-Level Leaders – Work to be the conductor among your team of leaders and not concern yourself with learning to play every instrument. This enables your people to develop the skills and experiences needed to address most issues limiting the amount they need to escalate to you to solve for them.

For Supervisory-Level Leaders – Don't rush to respond to every email. You could be cultivating dependencies on you within your team. Instead, encourage your team to ruminate on issues before they make them yours to solve.

Idea Crosswalk

- **Leadership Mindset** – When a leader prepares and empowers their teams, they can use silence as a tool.
- **Vision** – A vision that describes a workplace where leaders aren't expected to have all of the answers all of the time, attracts people who can work independently.
- **Company Culture** – An exceptional culture is one in which staffers are encouraged to solve problems without leaders guiding every step along the way.
- **Trust and Empowerment** – Silence can be used as a means of encouraging empowerment as leaders allow their people to figure things out without their immediate intervention.
- **Change Management** – Leaders can use silence to gauge the consensus of the group during major change activities.

All people are different people

Identifying each person's desires, skills and aptitudes is crucial to the superior performance of your team.

Guru Guidance

After providing feedback or coaching, allow a moment of silence for the team member to absorb the information and consider their next steps. This promotes self-reflection and personal growth.

Recognizing that people are different and have different needs and talents to contribute to the organization is a foundational element of effective leadership and is a key driver of business success.

> *" . . . distinguishing individual differences among your employees is essential for effective talent development . . . "*

In fact, it is essential that leaders use their understanding of each individual on their team to form the "right" combination of personalities for consistent execution. This enhances employee engagement, fosters creativity, and enriches the work experience for the entire team.

Additionally, when leaders acknowledge that people bring different things to the table, they are more likely to foster a culture that encourages creativity and fresh thinking. The most creative ideas often come from staffers who feel that their individual strengths and contributions are recognized and used by their leaders.

Unquestionably, distinguishing individual differences among your employees is essential for effective talent development, too. Leaders must be able to identify and nurture each staffer's unique talents, skills, and potential to help them grow and contribute to the success of the enterprise.

DOI: 10.4324/9781003422754-72

How to Put It into Action

For Executive-Level Leaders – Encourage your top leaders to mentor staffers within the organization. Ask them to seek out employees who are operating differently than they do. Direct them to create personal growth opportunities for those they are mentoring. This will reinforce the importance of "knowing" those whom they lead on an individual basis so to better inform and inspire.

For Mid-Level Leaders – Tailor your management and communication styles to suit each employee's needs and preferences. The practice creates greater employee engagement, job satisfaction, and productivity.

For Supervisory-Level Leaders – People will inevitably have different opinions and approaches to problem-solving. For a more harmonious work environment, use this knowledge of individual differences to better manage conflicts and discover resolutions that are more acceptable to each team member.

Idea Crosswalk

- **Leadership Mindset** – Understanding individual differences among staffers enables leaders to be more thoughtful and deliberate when forging new teams.
- **Vision** – Businesses that demonstrate a commitment to respecting individual differences and promoting diversity and inclusion are more positively viewed by customers and stakeholders. Be sure to include this sentiment in your vision story.
- **Company Culture** – Solid workplace cultures respect the "individual" and seek to leverage the strengths of the people who comprise the organization.
- **Trust and Empowerment** – Trust is enhanced when leaders offer flexible work arrangements to accommodate diverse needs, such as different family structures, health conditions, and other personal situations.
- **Change Management** – Train change management team leads to be cognizant of the fact that all people are different and that they may need to incorporate a variety of leadership styles in order to be most effective in driving change within the enterprise.

Ride your own ride

Exceptional leaders make their own decisions and live with the consequences.

Guru Guidance

Help your people recognize the responsibilities that they have to themselves and the organization by reminding them that the choices that they make each day have impact and resonance.

As a motorcycle rider, I know that this idea can literally save your life.

It infers that a rider must choose their own speed and make their own choices about when to pass and when to trail behind. In business, it refers to the need for a leader to decide on the correct course of action for them and their organization.

> *" . . . it refers to the need for a leader to decide on the correct course of action for them and their organization."*

Like a motorcyclist, a leader must gather the information available from their surroundings, identify the possibilities, determine the risks, and then take the action that they deem appropriate for the situation – anything less would be irresponsible and possibly catastrophic for them and the organization.

Indeed, following the crowd can be dangerous to the enterprise and limits groundbreaking thinking. Leaders who think for themselves, on the other hand, are more likely to come up with innovative and creative solutions to challenges. Their independent thinking promotes increased confidence by staffers in their leader's judgment and decisions, too.

Ultimately, it is a leader's job to be accountable for the decisions that they make and not take this responsibility lightly.

DOI: 10.4324/9781003422754-73

How to Put It into Action

For Executive-Level Leaders – Avoid blindly following trends or succumbing to external pressures that may compromise your ethical standards.

For Mid-Level Leaders – Don't fall prey to peer pressure or to your own insular tendencies. Instead, gather the courage needed to make the decision that you believe is right.

For Supervisory-Level Leaders – Approach problems from different angles before deciding on a course of action. This expands the palette of possibilities and improves your ability to make the right call.

Idea Crosswalk

- **Leadership Mindset** – Leaders who think for themselves are more likely to stand by their convictions, even in the face of opposition, which inspires confidence and trust among their team members.
- **Vision** – Winning enterprises don't feel compelled to adopt the same vision that your rivals are pursuing. You are not them.
- **Company Culture** – A culture that promotes independent thinking attracts top talent from all over the globe.
- **Trust and Empowerment** – Thinking independently allows leaders to evaluate risks objectively, considering potential outcomes and weighing the consequences of their decisions.
- **Change Management** – There are always several options available to drive change into an organization where better leaders take the time needed to determine the most appropriate tack to take.

Part V

Trust and Empowerment Tips

Indispensable leaders know what it takes to win. They encourage their people to work together, and they cultivate trust through their words and actions.

They invest in developing their people so they can be empowered. Employees who feel supported and empowered are more likely to stick around. When people stick around they can be groomed for future leadership roles.

They recognize that people need autonomy. Autonomy enables employees to gain a sense of ownership for their work and that leads to increased motivation and engagement.

These tips help leaders deliver results by developing trust in their people and empowering them to do their best work.

DOI: 10.4324/9781003422754-74

Everything you're doing is preparing you for what comes next

When leaders acknowledge their own growth journey and the lessons they've learned along the way, it establishes their authenticity and builds trust within the enterprise.

Guru Guidance

Employees are more likely to trust leaders who are open about their experiences and challenges. It humanizes them, making them more relatable to staff members. This drives the kind of deep connection that carries weight, especially during challenging times, when trust is most needed.

Recognizing that leadership is a journey of learning and growth makes leaders more empathetic and understanding towards their employees. They are better able to relate to the challenges and setbacks staffers encounter, which, in turn, builds trust.

Similarly, staff members are more likely to trust leaders who share their own growth journey. When leaders acknowledge how their past experiences prepared them for what they're doing now, it instills confidence in their decisions.

> " . . . leaders who embrace the idea that everything they do contributes to the development of others tend to be more thoughtful and deliberate in their actions . . . "

Likewise, leaders who embrace the idea that everything they do contributes to the development of others tend to be more thoughtful and deliberate in their actions, which strengthens the trust that others have in them.

Indeed, leaders who operate with this level of self-awareness and share their experiences with colleagues with the intent to make them better, tend to be respected and gain hardy "followership."

DOI: 10.4324/9781003422754-75

How to Put It into Action

For Executive-Level Leaders – Discuss the challenges you've faced, what you've learned from those experiences, and how you've used those lessons to improve. This helps your top leaders see that they are on a continuous journey of development, too.

For Mid-Level Leaders – Seek out mentorship and coaching from others. This shows that you recognize the importance of learning from others and continuously improving your skills.

For Supervisory-Level Leaders – Reflect on your past experiences, both successes and failures. It helps you to extract valuable lessons and insights. Sharing these reflections with your team conveys a commitment to learning from the past and using those lessons for the future.

Idea Crosswalk

- **Leadership Mindset** – Leaders who encourage employees to embrace challenges and continuously improve their skills by sharing how they've done the same in their careers inspire greatness in others.
- **Vision** – Recognizing that current actions are preparation for the future ensures that leaders' decisions and strategies are aligned with the long-term vision and goals of the organization.
- **Company Culture** – Leaders who acknowledge that everything they do contributes to their development help foster a culture of growth and learning within the enterprise.
- **People and Talent** – Leaders who recognize the importance of personal development for themselves are more likely to prioritize employee development within the organization.
- **Change Management** – Leaders who view every experience as preparation for the future are better equipped to manage change within the organization. This mindset helps staffers navigate change more effectively, too.

Exceptional leaders keep calm and carry on

By maintaining your composure, resilience, and ability to make effective decisions in the face of challenges, inspires greatness in your people.

Guru Guidance

Your ability to handle tough situations with grace encourages others to persevere and stay committed to the organization's mission. It is a hallmark of a remarkable leader.

> *"By maintaining your composure, you put others at ease."*

Exceptional leaders set the tone for their teams. By remaining calm in the face of adversity, they demonstrate resilience and composure, inspiring their team members to do the same. When leaders remain calm, they can think more clearly and make better decisions. Emotional reactions cloud judgment, while a calm demeanor enables a more rational and strategic approach to problem-solving.

Likewise, during times of crisis or uncertainty, employees and stakeholders tend to feel anxious and overwhelmed. A composed leader provides a sense of stability and reassurance, which helps maintain trust and confidence in the organization. By maintaining your composure, you put others at ease.

Equally, exceptional leaders are resilient and can bounce back from setbacks and challenges. Despite obvious obstacles, their ability to keep moving forward inspires resilience in others, as well. Staying calm helps leaders maintain their focus on the most critical priorities, and not get distracted by fear or anxiety.

DOI: 10.4324/9781003422754-76

How to Put It into Action

For Executive-Level Leaders – Reflect on past experiences, especially those in which you successfully remained calm in challenging situations. Use these lessons to reinforce your ability to keep calm in the future.

For Mid-Level Leaders – Anticipate potential challenges and develop contingency plans. Being well-prepared can reduce anxiety and increase your confidence.

For Supervisory-Level Leaders – Incorporate mindfulness practices or stress management techniques into your daily routine. These can help you stay composed under pressure.

Idea Crosswalk

- **Leadership Mindset** – Top leaders view pressure and challenges as opportunities for growth.
- **Vision** – Maintaining calm under pressure helps leaders to stay focused, enabling them to be less likely to make impulsive decisions that deviate from the organization's strategic vision.
- **Company Culture** – A leader's composure in challenging situations helps to shape a more resilient organizational culture – one that handles pressure with poise and determination.
- **People and Talent** – Leaders who are calm, cool, and collected are better positioned to provide needed reassurance, guidance, and support to stressed-out staffers.
- **Change Management** – Leaders who remain unruffled when things don't go as planned will lead teams through change with confidence and clarity, minimizing resistance and ensuring a smoother transition into the future.

It's cool to be kind

Showing kindness through what you say and do creates a positive and high-trust work environment.

Guru Guidance

Kindness is not just a personal virtue; it can also be a strategic advantage for businesses looking to thrive and flourish over time.

Being kind is "cool" because it leads to a better workplace, improved employee morale, and positive relationships with key stakeholders.

For instance, your staffers are more likely to feel happy and satisfied in their roles when they have a leader who genuinely cares about their well-being. When leaders exhibit kindness in thought and deed, they boost team morale and inspire trust.

> *"When leaders exhibit kindness in thought and deed, they boost team morale and inspire trust."*

As mentioned, kindness should be extended to customers and other key stakeholders, too. Treating customers with respect and consideration, for example, creates positive customer experiences, greater customer intimacy and stronger brand loyalty.

Indeed, a leadership team that routinely exhibits kindness brings about a more positive reputation in the marketplace. This characteristic attracts clients, investors, and partners, alike.

Consider kindness as a long-term strategy for business success. It may not yield immediate results, but over time, it can lead to a more loyal workforce, stronger customer relationships, and rampant growth.

How to Put It into Action

For Executive-Level Leaders – Ensure that you treat all team members fairly and equally, regardless of their background, gender, or other

DOI: 10.4324/9781003422754-77

characteristics. Kindness includes promoting a workplace that is free from discrimination and bias.

For Mid-Level Leaders – When conflicts or challenges arise, approach them with a problem-solving mindset. Trust is enhanced when you work collaboratively with your team of leaders to find solutions that benefit everyone.

For Supervisory-Level Leaders – Kindness fosters trust and loyalty among employees. Treat your people with respect and understanding, for it leads to greater employee satisfaction, retention, and productivity.

Idea Crosswalk

- **Leadership Mindset** – Kindness is a leadership mentality that has a positive impact on the overall leadership philosophy within an enterprise.
- **Vision** – A vision that incorporates kindness may focus on creating a positive impact on society, fostering strong relationships with stakeholders, and contributing to a better world.
- **Company Culture** – Kindness is a foundational element in shaping a company's culture. A leader who embodies kindness and understanding fosters a culture of respect, collaboration, and employee well-being.
- **People and Talent** – Talent management strategies should include leadership development programs that accentuate the emotional intelligence and interpersonal skills of staffers.
- **Change Management** – Change frameworks must be built around principles of kindness, transparency, and inclusion, which lead to greater employee buy-in.

Incessantly train them up!

Continuous preparation helps teams adapt to evolving circumstances, including changes in the organization, business environment and customer demands.

Guru Guidance

Training is an investment that you're making in your organization's success. By being better prepared for the unexpected, teams can identify and mitigate potential risks and issues before they escalate. This reduces the likelihood of major disruptions or costly mistakes in execution.

Prepared personnel are better equipped to pivot and adjust to new challenges and opportunities.

> *" . . . better preparedness reduces uncertainty and anxiety among team members."*

The marketplace is dynamic. A well-trained workforce is more agile and responsive to changes and market opportunities. This can give the organization a competitive advantage by allowing it to act swiftly and stay ahead of competitors.

The better prepared, the better the decision-making. When staffers have the information and tools needed to make well-informed choices, their execution is enhanced.

Indeed, better preparedness reduces uncertainty and anxiety among team members. This not only improves their individual well-being but also ensures that they can execute tasks at a high level while under stress.

Continual preparation can provide team members with opportunities for personal and professional growth, too. This contributes to greater job satisfaction and enhances their ability to delight the customer.

DOI: 10.4324/9781003422754-78

How to Put It into Action

For Executive-Level Leaders – Invest in ongoing training and development programs to enhance your employee's skills and knowledge. Provide opportunities for growth and learning through the implementation of a robust talent development program.

For Mid-Level Leaders – Provide mentorship and coaching to your team of leaders, helping them develop their skills and grow professionally.

For Supervisory-Level Leaders – Encourage your team to take ownership of their work and make decisions within their areas of responsibility. This inspires them to become better prepared and more accountable.

Idea Crosswalk

- **Leadership Mindset** – The leader who values constant preparation boosts learning, development, and commitment among staffers.
- **Vision** – When a leader consistently prepares their staffers for better performance, they reinforce the company's vision.
- **Company Culture** – The leader's commitment to ongoing development fosters a culture of proactivity, continuous improvement, and adaptability.
- **People and Talent** – A leader's focus on continual preparation contributes to their people's ability to meet evolving performance expectations.
- **Change Management** – Leaders who prioritize training are more effective at implementing change initiatives.

Don't fear asking!

It's a way to gain additional perspective, shows humility and builds trust and respect among peers.

Guru Guidance

Some leaders feel like they must "go it alone." Regularly remind your people that this is a losing mindset. Teach them that it's important to ask for assistance when needed.

None of us have all of the answers. Leaders should not feel that they are any different just because of their role or title.

For this reason, we should all feel comfortable asking for advice – even from those on our team.

In fact, when you do, you're demonstrating that you are down-to-earth, approachable and authentic. After all, someone who is willing to ask for advice is a person who isn't pretending to be someone that they are not.

> *" . . . you can ask for help and demonstrate modesty, while forging stronger bonds among your contemporaries."*

Further, seeking assistance from others also provides you with additional perspectives that can prove valuable when problem-solving, while fostering a deeper connection with coworkers. This helps to build mutual trust and respect.

Lastly, because the practice is effective with colleagues from all levels of an organization, you can ask for help and demonstrate modesty, while forging stronger bonds among your contemporaries.

How to Put It into Action

For Executive-Level Leaders – There is immense bonding power that comes when asking someone for advice. Use it with people whom you want to get closer to. Asking a peer for a book, movie, or restaurant

DOI: 10.4324/9781003422754-79

recommendation, for instance, is an easy way to get started. It can turn a rival into a friend!

For Mid-Level Leaders – Don't beat around the bush by asking for general advice. You want your request to be personal and specific. It shows respect for the other person and saves them from expending cycles considering vague questions.

For Supervisory-Level Leaders – Stay away from asking for advice on hypothetical situations. It can feel like a quiz to your staffers and, often, comes across as disingenuous.

Idea Crosswalk

- **Leadership Mindset** – Being comfortable asking for help makes most leadership challenges easier to manage.
- **Vision** – Leaders who regularly solicit input from peers help to establish a work environment that enables vision achievement.
- **Company Culture** – A culture that features open communication and strong collegial relationships tends to attract talented people who are energized by being on successful teams.
- **People and Talent** – Leaders who don't shy away from asking for help when needed demonstrate that no one is expected to have all of the answers.
- **Change Management** – Change management initiatives tend to be more successful when staffers learn to ask questions without fear of reprisal.

All you can do is your best

To maximize the trust-building potential of the phrase, it must be accompanied by actions that align with its spirit.

Guru Guidance

In practice, "doing your best" means consistently giving your greatest effort, being accountable for your actions, communicating openly, and fostering a culture of excellence and collaboration.

The phrase "all you can do is your best" can be a powerful tool in building trust within an organization when it is applied in a meaningful and consistent way.

Basically, A strong work ethic is a fundamental component of trust. When individuals consistently put in their best effort and demonstrate a commitment to their work, it reflects positively on their character and appeal.

> *"Demonstrating a commitment to giving your best effort inspires confidence . . . "*

Indeed, people tend to trust individuals who are knowledgeable and skilled in their roles. So, consistently striving for excellence and putting forth one's best effort will lead to the further development of expertise and credibility for yourself and serve to "feed the fire" for excellence among contemporaries.

Further, establishing confidence in a team's capabilities (when everyone on the team is committed to doing their best) is a significant factor in trust-building, as well. You inspire confidence and improve the organization's capacity to achieve its goals, when you try your best.

Accordingly, when everyone within an organization is encouraged to do their best, it fosters a culture of collaboration and support. Trust is built when team members know they can count on each other to get the work done.

DOI: 10.4324/9781003422754-80

How to Put It into Action

For **Executive-Level Leaders** – Demonstrate your commitment to do your best by maintaining consistency in decision-making. It shows that you are reliable and dependable, which fosters trust in you among your team of top leaders.

For **Mid-Level Leaders** – Be accountable for your actions by acknowledging mistakes, and by taking responsibility for finding the solutions required to correct them.

For **Supervisory-Level Leaders** – Offer guidance and support to help team members reach their full potential. The most effective leaders are the ones who empower their people by providing opportunities for growth and development.

Idea Crosswalk

- **Leadership Mindset** – Making a commitment to do one's best helps to shape the organization's leadership philosophy by prioritizing integrity, fairness, and work ethic.
- **Vision** – Leaders who strive to do their best set high standards for themselves and their staffers, which is a key characteristic of any organization's vision.
- **Company Culture** – Leaders who consistently give their best contribute to a culture that values excellence – one that encourages employees to excel and take pride in their work.
- **People and Talent** – Employees are more likely to trust and respect leaders who model dedication, which usually leads to increased loyalty and commitment from the workforce.
- **Change Management** – Leaders who are committed to bringing their best to the workplace every day facilitate a smoother transition during periods of change.

Genuine humility disarms the critics

The practice leads to more productive and satisfying work relationships and staffer interactions.

Guru Guidance

When leaders approach criticism or challenges with humility, they are more likely to defuse tension, build trust, and create a collaborative atmosphere where constructive solutions can be explored and implemented – leading to more positive outcomes and stronger relationships within the organization.

Genuine humility demonstrates self-awareness and a balanced understanding of one's strengths and weaknesses. Higher self-awareness makes a person appear more grounded and relatable, as they acknowledge their imperfections and limitations.

Undoubtedly, humble people are less likely to become defensive when faced with criticism or challenges. Instead of reacting with arrogance or dismissiveness, they are open to feedback and willing to consider alternative perspectives, which set a higher bar for others to clear.

> *" . . . practicing humility tends to create a more collaborative and team-oriented work environment."*

Also, modesty goes hand-in-hand with empathy. When someone is genuinely humble, they are more likely to understand and appreciate the feelings and viewpoints of others, including their critics. This empathetic approach can lead to more constructive and respectful business relationships.

At the end of the day, a self-effacing response to criticism is a sign of respect for the person offering the critique. Acknowledging the validity of someone's perspective and showing appreciation for their input can defuse tension and build goodwill. In fact, practicing humility tends to create a more collaborative and team-oriented work environment.

DOI: 10.4324/9781003422754-81

Thus, work on acting humbly and demonstrate your willingness to cooperate with your critics to find common ground and reach solutions that benefit everyone.

How to Put It into Action

For Executive-Level Leaders – Work on being more flexible in your direction-setting. Humble leaders are open to change and adaptation. They recognize that they don't have all the answers and are willing to adjust their strategies as necessary.

For Mid-Level Leaders – Demonstrate patience and understanding, especially when dealing with challenges and conflicts. Show your people that you possess the humility they're looking for in their leader.

For Supervisory-Level Leaders – Make yourself accessible and approachable to team members, and encourage open communication and collaboration. Approachability is a key aspect of unpretentiousness.

Idea Crosswalk

- **Leadership Mindset** – Leaders who practice humility have a transformative impact on their organizations by fostering a culture of trust, collaboration, and openness.
- **Vision** – Highlighting humble leadership makes a strategic vision more compelling.
- **Company Culture** – Unassuming leaders value different perspectives and encourage a culture where all voices are heard and respected.
- **People and Talent** – Leaders who demonstrate modesty usually excel in conflict resolution. They facilitate constructive discussions, encourage compromise, and work to find solutions that benefit everyone involved.
- **Change Management** – Humble leaders build trust during times of change. Their transparent communication style and willingness to admit when they make mistakes create a sense of security during organizational transformation initiatives.

If you want to be a better leader, change your mind

The best leaders make mid-course adjustments to improve their team's chances for success.

Guru Guidance

Fold adaptability into your leadership repertoire. A willingness to course-correct helps an organization maintain momentum and inspires staffers to take a fresh look at what they can do to accelerate execution.

Healthy organizations are dynamic. Economic conditions, market trends, and competition rapidly change, and enterprises must change accordingly. It is essential that leaders adapt their plans to remain competitive. If they don't, they will fail.

> *"It is essential that leaders adapt their plans to remain competitive."*

In fact, as leaders gather more information, they may uncover insights that necessitate a change in direction. Often, enhanced situational awareness is derived from customer feedback, performance metrics, and new research findings. Sometimes the need for course correction is indicated simply by unexpected situations emerging in the marketplace.

Of course, input from employees, customers, or stakeholders provides valuable insights, as well. Leaders who are open to this kind of feedback are more successful because they are more willing to adjust strategies to improve outcomes.

Indeed, leaders must be ready to adapt and modify their strategies to overcome unforeseen challenges and obstacles. After all, things change and plans need to change, too.

DOI: 10.4324/9781003422754-82

How to Put It into Action

For Executive-Level Leaders – Be sure to put solid strategy governance processes in place to ensure that you are receiving the "right information" at the "right time" to make adjustments in a sensible and effective way.

For Mid-Level Leaders – When the new information suggests that a mid-course adjustment is needed, act quickly. Work to reallocate personnel, and budgets, and focus on activities that promise better outcomes. Be sure to communicate the "why" as you implement these changes to your team of leaders, too.

For Supervisory-Level Leaders – Adapt to changing circumstances by making timely decisions on issues brought forward to you by your team. After all, even if the change in direction fails to reap obvious benefits, sometimes it's better to ask for forgiveness than to wait for permission.

Idea Crosswalk

- **Leadership Mindset** – Leadership mindset and approach play a critical role in determining how mid-course adjustments are made and communicated throughout the enterprise.
- **Vision** – Mid-course adjustments should be aligned with this vision to ensure that changes in strategy do not deviate from the overall purpose and direction of the organization.
- **Company Culture** – Changes in direction should be made in a way that aligns with the organization's culture to maintain consistency and employee morale.
- **People and Talent** – Leaders need to ensure that their teams understand the reasons behind changes in strategies and are given the necessary support and resources to successfully make any course corrections.
- **Change Management** – Leaders of change initiatives must plan, communicate, and execute changes effectively while minimizing resistance and disruption.

You don't learn much from only listening to yourself!

Listening to others' feedback and insights provides leaders with a more balanced and objective view of their actions and ideas.

Guru Guidance

Effective leadership involves understanding and empathizing with the needs, concerns, and viewpoints of others. Asking for input and listening to others is essential to gaining a fuller understanding of what is needed in any given situation.

To be most effective, it's important for leaders to actively seek out diverse viewpoints, listen to others, and engage in open dialogue. There is much to learn from the feedback, perspectives, and information gleaned from the people that are actually doing the work.

> *"There is a much to learn from the feedback, perspectives and information gleaned from the people that are actually doing the work."*

What's more, listening to others' feedback and insights can provide leaders with a more balanced and objective view of their own thinking and provide the fodder needed to change one's mind for the better.

Let's not forget that our confirmation bias can be bad for business, as well. Only focusing on information that aligns with our own existing beliefs puts our organizations at risk. Indeed, we can miss out on innovative ideas, alternative strategies, or market insights that could offer better ways of setting direction for the enterprise.

Moreover, besides stifling creativity and innovation, ignoring information that contradicts one's beliefs often results in poor decision-making – and that can lead to catastrophic results for an organization.

DOI: 10.4324/9781003422754-83

How to Put It into Action

For **Executive-Level Leaders** – Express gratitude and appreciation for the feedback you receive. Let people know that their opinions are valued and that their input can lead to positive changes.

For **Mid-Level Leaders** – When appropriate, act on the feedback that you receive from your team of leaders. Address concerns, make necessary changes, and communicate the steps you've taken to address their feedback. This demonstrates your commitment to improvement.

For **Supervisory-Level Leaders** – Reflect on the feedback received. Analyze common themes and patterns. Consider the changes that you might want to make in your leadership mindset and decision-making approach.

Idea Crosswalk

- **Leadership Mindset** – Leaders who actively seek opinions and feedback cultivate a winning mindset – one open to new ideas and acting on emerging opportunities.
- **Vision** – Leaders who are open to new ways of thinking and doing ensure that the organization's strategic vision remains relevant and adaptable to changing circumstances.
- **Company Culture** – Leaders who actively seek feedback contribute to the creation of a culture that celebrates collaboration, communication transparency, and continuous improvement.
- **People and Talent** – Seeking feedback is a fundamental aspect of effective people management. It involves understanding the needs and concerns of team members, demonstrating empathy, and addressing issues that may be affecting their performance or well-being.
- **Change Management** – Feedback is a valuable component of all change frameworks. It helps leaders assess the impact of changes, identify obstacles, and make necessary adjustments to ensure successful change implementation.

Listen to understand, not to respond

Listening to understand allows leaders to gain valuable insights into the issues faced by their employees.

Guru Guidance

Miscommunications and misunderstandings happen when we prioritize crafting a response over understanding what is being messaged to us. This leads to problems and inefficiencies within an organization. By listening to understand, leaders reduce the risk of misinterpretation and prevent unnecessary conflicts.

> *"When employees feel heard and understood, they come to trust their leaders . . . "*

When people are more focused on their own viewpoint and response, they are dismissing and invalidating the perspectives of others. This can create a trying and uncooperative workplace.

The impact can be catastrophic for an organization.

Over time, leaders who fail to listen erode trust. Their staffers begin to believe them to be self-centered and disinterested in what others have to say.

On the other hand, when leaders actively listen to their staffers, it shows that they value their opinions and perspectives. This nurtures trust and respect within an enterprise. When employees feel heard and understood, they come to trust their leaders and collaborate openly with them.

Further, a leader who shows that they are genuinely interested in what their people have to say helps to build employee self-confidence. This results in better problem-solving, innovation, and collaboration across the organization.

Clearly, by simply listening, leaders can create a powerful and effective trust dynamic within their organizations – improving communication, interpersonal relationships, and business results. So, listen up and everybody wins!

DOI: 10.4324/9781003422754-84

How to Put It into Action

For Executive-Level Leaders – Practice active listening! Active listening involves not only hearing the words but also understanding the emotions and intentions behind them. Nodding, paraphrasing, and reflecting on what the speaker is saying are all components of active listening.

For Mid-Level Leaders – Refrain from interrupting a colleague, even if you have an urge to respond or provide solutions. Let them finish their thoughts and express their ideas before offering your perspective.

For Supervisory-Level Leaders – When someone is speaking to you, make a conscious effort to give them your full attention. This means putting away distractions, making eye contact, and showing through body language that you are fully engaged in the conversation.

Idea Crosswalk

- **Leadership Mindset** – When leaders actively listen and seek to understand, they build trust and credibility across the enterprise.
- **Vision** – Effective listening helps leaders gain insights into the needs, concerns, and aspirations of their employees, which can be used to inform their vision for the organization.
- **Company Culture** – A culture of listening and understanding fortifies teamwork, cooperation, and collaboration among the workforce.
- **People and Talent** – Leaders who listen for understanding are better equipped to improve people strategies related to training, coaching, and career progression.
- **Change Management** – When employees feel that their concerns and input are considered during times of change, they are more likely to buy into change initiatives.

Sometimes you just need to get out of the way!

Allowing well-prepared team members to take the lead empowers them and fosters their sense of ownership over the work.

Guru Guidance

Training is an important element of staff preparedness. Don't empower them until you are confident that they have been properly developed to put them in charge of making the call.

Leaders should get out of the way when their team members are fully prepared to perform because it promotes empowerment, autonomy, skills utilization, morale, and innovation. It allows leaders to focus on higher-level responsibilities like strategy-setting and workplace optimization.

Let's face it, able staffers are often best equipped to make decisions and execute tasks autonomously. When leaders step back, it allows their people to exercise their skills and judgment. This improves efficiency and eliminates bottlenecks that come when staffers are made to traverse too many layers of management to gain approval.

> *"When leaders step back, it allows their people to exercise their skills and judgment."*

Besides, empowered staffers tend to have higher morale and motivation. People have greater job satisfaction when they feel that their leaders trust them. In fact, too much leader involvement in the daily work of a well-prepared team only leads to team member burnout.

Indeed, leaders can create a culture that values autonomy, fosters leadership development, and inspires greater accountability by simply allowing properly prepared teams to take the lead. This not only enhances individual growth but also leads to better success in the marketplace.

DOI: 10.4324/9781003422754-85

How to Put It into Action

For Executive-Level Leaders – Hold team members accountable for their performance and decisions. Encourage them to take responsibility for their work by stepping out of the way.

For Mid-Level Leaders – Provide the necessary resources, tools, and support to enable team members to succeed independently.

For Supervisory-Level Leaders – Clearly define roles, responsibilities, and expectations. Delegate tasks to team members based on their skills and expertise.

Idea Crosswalk

- **Leadership Mindset** – A leader must recognize that getting out of the way of a well-prepared team is fundamental for the company's long-term success and its ability to thrive in an ever-changing business environment.
- **Vision** – Charging well-prepared staffers to take the reins reinforces a vision that highlights empowerment and execution.
- **Company Culture** – A brilliant culture emerges when individuals are encouraged to take ownership of their work, collaborate, and actively contribute to the organization's success.
- **People and Talent** – Effective people management involves creating a work environment where individuals are valued and empowered. It demonstrates trust in their abilities and encourages their growth and development.
- **Change Management** – Empowered employees are more likely to embrace change, contribute innovative ideas, and actively participate in the implementation of new ways of doing business.

Don't ever throw your people under the bus

When employees know that their leaders have their backs, they are more likely to own up to mistakes.

Guru Guidance

Supporting team members when they make mistakes builds trust and creates psychological safety within the organization – this is foundational in building an enterprise that consistently delivers outstanding results.

Leaders, who stand by their people, even when they make mistakes, create a culture of trust, learning, and resilience. In the long run, having your people's backs improves their overall performance and drives the success of the organization.

> *"Remember, mistakes provide valuable learning opportunities."*

Remember, mistakes provide valuable learning opportunities. By supporting individuals through their mistakes, leaders can help them understand what went wrong, why it happened, and how to prevent similar errors in the future – and these kinds of "learning organizations" regularly outperform the competition.

Further, working through mistakes promotes the development of problem-solving skills. Team members learn to analyze situations, identify root causes, and find effective solutions. This enhances their ability to handle challenges in the future.

Leaders encourage creativity and a willingness to experiment among their staffers when they forge a supportive work environment. After all, a workplace that penalizes mistakes only stifles innovation. Hence, be prepared to stand with your people even when they occasionally slip up.

DOI: 10.4324/9781003422754-86

How to Put It into Action

For Executive-Level Leaders – Foster a learning environment where mistakes are seen as opportunities for growth. Encourage continuous development and improvement.

For Mid-Level Leaders – While it's essential to support team members during mistakes, also ensure that accountability is balanced. In cases of repeated or serious mistakes, address them appropriately while creating opportunities to provide hands-on coaching, as needed.

For Supervisory-Level Leaders – Recognize and appreciate the effort and intentions of team members, even if the outcomes are not as expected. Highlight the value of taking initiative and trying one's best.

Idea Crosswalk

- **Leadership Mindset** – A leader's willingness to support their people, even when they make mistakes, is intrinsically connected to a company's ability to exceed all stakeholder expectations.
- **Vision** – Supporting team members through their mistakes aligns with a company's vision that promotes continuous improvement.
- **Company Culture** – Leaders who support their people when they make mistakes help to establish a culture of learning and growth.
- **People and Talent** – Effective people management involves creating a workplace where team members are valued, supported, and trusted.
- **Change Management** – Exhibiting a high level of staffer support is vital to ensure a smooth transition during periods of great change.

Stop making excuses for failing!

All of our excuses are just lies that we tell ourselves to feel better.

Guru Guidance

By accepting failure as a part of the leadership journey, leaders can flip the script of their self-talk and, ultimately, become more effective in their roles.

Failure is a natural part of any leadership role. When leaders make excuses for their failures, they miss out on valuable learning opportunities. Embracing failure, on the other hand, allows leaders to learn from their mistakes, adapt, and grow both personally and professionally.

As a leader, organizational accountability begins with you! If you can't face the facts, how can you expect your team to overcome the inevitability that sometimes they will fall short of expectations?

> *"As a leader, organizational accountability begins with you!"*

It's up to us to establish the right frame of mind to accept our mistakes. When leaders own up to their failures and take responsibility, it encourages a culture of accountability. This, in turn, emboldens team members to take ownership of their mistakes and learn from them, too. The most exceptional leaders among us, in fact, will tell you that things failed because "I didn't do my job."

Remember that being accountable is a forever thing. It's about consistently demonstrating the values and behaviors that promote responsibility and integrity within your organization. When you do, you help to create a workplace where everyone takes ownership of their actions and contributes to the overall success of the enterprise.

DOI: 10.4324/9781003422754-87

How to Put It into Action

For Executive-Level Leaders – Practice self-reflection by giving yourself some time every day to consider how you're doing. It can help you to (re)solve some of your current challenges without feeling compelled to form excuses for failings.

For Mid-Level Leaders – Encourage team members to hold each other accountable through peer reviews and "accountability partnerships" (a practice where colleagues agree to hold each other accountable for following through on commitments made to the enterprise).

For Supervisory-Level Leaders – When you commit to something, ensure you follow through. This not only shows accountability but also builds trust within your team.

Idea Crosswalk

- **Leadership Mindset** – Top leadership's willingness to accept accountability sets the tone for an organization's leadership ethos. When a leader is willing to be accountable for their actions and decisions, it helps to build a culture of responsibility and integrity.
- **Vision** – The leader's actions and decisions should support the broader vision, and their accountability ensures that they are working towards the vision's realization.
- **Company Culture** – When leaders take responsibility for their failures and encourage others to do the same, it leads to the creation of a culture of higher trust and greater transparency.
- **People and Talent** – When a leader is accountable, it stimulates trust and respect among team members. This, in turn, positively impacts people management, as employees are more likely to follow a leader who demonstrates accountability and treats others with respect.
- **Change Management** – Accountability in change management involves open and honest communication about the reasons for changes, potential obstacles, and the way forward.

Do not take stock of criticism from a person that you wouldn't ask for advice

Be leery of accepting unsolicited feedback from a colleague that you don't know or respect.

Guru Guidance

Trust your gut! Ultimately, you have the responsibility to make decisions that are in the best interest of your organization. If, after careful consideration, you still find the advice you're receiving to be questionable, trust your instincts and do what you think is right.

> *" . . . proceed with caution. Ulterior motives may be at play."*

Take a moment and think back on your life. Identify the people that truly made a difference to you. I bet they were people who had your best interest in mind. I bet they were people who you came to respect.

Because of these characteristics, the feedback that they offered, while sometimes tough to swallow, was always accepted and reflected upon by you over time. You would take it to heart, for example, when a respected family member, teacher, or coach offered an opinion aimed at making you better.

However, sometimes a person that you don't know, or respect offers uninvited advice or criticism under the guise of being helpful. It's in these times that you must proceed with caution. Ulterior motives may be at play and those motives may be impossible to discern at face value.

Remember, you have the right to decide what weight you give anyone's critique of you. If you wouldn't ask this person for advice, why would you accept their criticism?

How to Put It into Action

For **Executive-Level Leaders** – When someone offers you unsolicited advice, say thanks and move on. It sets a tone. However, it doesn't

DOI: 10.4324/9781003422754-88

become something that requires follow-up or further action. Unless you think that there's something to be gained by further considering what has been offered.

For Mid-Level Leaders – We all have blind spots that others can help to illuminate. Don't be afraid to seek out advice and opinions from those you know and respect. But don't give too much credence to advice given by someone who might not have your best interests in mind.

For Supervisory-Level Leaders – It's OK to ask for more elaboration and details whenever someone is providing feedback to you. It's the best way to fully grasp the thoughts that the person has to offer. Just be sure to take note of "from whence it comes."

Idea Crosswalk

- **Leadership Mindset** – When a leader refuses unsolicited advice from someone they don't respect, it is often a sign of strong and decisive leadership.
- **Vision** – Declining uninvited advice that is not aligned with the organization's vision or strategy can help maintain a clear and consistent vision.
- **Company Culture** – Decisive leadership can help in implementing cultural changes efficiently and in accordance with the desired outcome.
- **People and Talent** – Employees may learn when to provide input and when to respect the boundaries set by their leader. This understanding can help in their professional development and align with the organization's ideals.
- **Change Management** – During change efforts, declining unsolicited advice that deviates from the strategic intent of the initiative can help to minimize confusion and maintain focus on delivering anticipated outcomes.

Time is your friend!

Use time wisely and make it a tool that you can bend to your advantage.

Guru Guidance

A leader who recognizes and utilizes time as a valuable resource is better able to promote strategic thinking, patience, learning, resilience, and innovation among their people.

Time can be a friend to leaders because it can be used to create opportunities for growth, learning, and relationship-building. The most skilled leaders recognize the value of time and use it to their advantage in order to make a lasting, positive impact on their organizations.

Often, you need time to properly collaborate and to decide how to address issues and questions as they arise. It's essential that you make time for yourself and your team to think things through and not feel compelled to craft a solution at a moment's notice.

> *"Remember, challenges often work themselves out . . . "*

Remember, challenges often work themselves out without any intervention on your part – you just need to give those situations some time to change. Using time to your advantage takes practice. But, over the long haul, it will help you to develop better decision-making instincts.

Indeed, time can be a friend if you use it wisely. So, resist always being in a mad rush to immediately *"fix"* every trial and tribulation that springs up. Instead, make a commitment to giving things time. It is an investment that you're making in yourself and your team, which pays dividends in the form of a better-performing enterprise.

How to Put It into Action

For Executive-Level Leaders – Be sure to manage expectations and control the messaging related to what you expect as a "timely response" to

DOI: 10.4324/9781003422754-89

your requests. Because you set the tone for timeliness, most staffers will respond immediately to your missives, unless you say otherwise. So, let them know what the acceptable turnaround time is for responding to your questions.

For Mid-Level Leaders – Your team of leaders must be encouraged to take the time required to collaborate and determine an appropriate course of action before engaging you in the process. Be sure to communicate this expectation.

For Supervisory-Level Leaders – Pace yourself and your team's response to newly emerging issues and requests for action. Not every issue and request is urgent. Take the time to think things through. It will also provide a period for things to get sorted out on their own.

Idea Crosswalk

- **Leadership Mindset** – A leader who uses their time to their advantage is more likely to maintain a steady and consistent approach to leadership.
- **Vision** – Patience is an essential underpinning of a strategic vision that supports long-term thinking.
- **Company Culture** – A leader who values the use of time as an asset can instill patience and resilience within the organization's culture.
- **People and Talent** – Leaders who understand the value of time can encourage teams to experiment and iterate, fostering a culture of innovation and creativity.
- **Change Management** – When managing change, a leader who uses time to plan and execute changes thoughtfully can minimize disruptions and resistance later on.

Make encouragement a superpower

It's amazing what people can achieve by simply cheering them on.

Guru Guidance

Encouragement and support from a leader can lead to increased loyalty from team members, as they feel a deep sense of appreciation and connection. Often, it is all that is needed to inspire greatness.

In essence, a leader's encouragement serves as a catalyst for human potential. It taps into the intrinsic motivation of individuals, helping them believe in themselves and their abilities. It can transform what might initially seem impossible into a challenge that is worth pursuing with determination and dedication.

> *"... don't be in a hurry to explain every nuance or implication."*

Providing direction is often needed to ensure success. However, give too much direction at the wrong time, and you become a micromanager. So, be careful and thoughtful in your direction-setting.

Yes, it is important to be clear and concise when giving direction and addressing issues. But don't be in a hurry to explain every nuance or implication of what you just directed. Encourage your people to think for themselves. They will ask questions when they don't understand something.

Accordingly, examine each situation to determine what your team needs to be successful. Often, your encouragement is all that is required. This is particularly true in instances where they know their stuff and just need to be reminded that they can get the job done on their own.

Indeed, when a leader provides encouragement, it boosts the confidence of personnel. Believing that someone in a position of authority has faith in their abilities can instill the self-assurance needed to take on any business challenges that they happen to confront.

DOI: 10.4324/9781003422754-90

How to Put It into Action

For Executive-Level Leaders – Be clear in setting your expectations for your organization. Be less directive about how those expectations should be met. Let your people determine the "how to."

For Mid-Level Leaders – Exercise restraint when you're feeling compelled to explain every step to be followed by your team of leaders. If more direction is needed, they will ask.

For Supervisory-Level Leaders – Pay close attention to every leadership situation. Learn when your team needs your direction and when your encouragement is all that is required. Practice giving your team what they need, when they need it. This will make you a better leader in the long run and it will help them to develop the confidence that they need to excel.

Idea Crosswalk

- **Leadership Mindset** – A leader's willingness to provide encouragement can be a powerful driving force within any enterprise.
- **Vision** – Leaders who encourage their employees to achieve the "*impossible*" set high expectations that should be reflected in the organization's vision story.
- **Company Culture** – Leaders who provide reassurance during tough times create a supportive and nurturing culture where staffers feel safe and secure.
- **People and Talent** – Encouragement reinforces the belief that challenges can be overcome. It fosters a "*can-do*" attitude, which is essential for tackling obstacles that appear seemingly insurmountable at first blush.
- **Change Management** – Encouragement signals that a desired change is possible and that team members have the support needed to adapt to it successfully.

You don't have to win every time

Certain leaders are inherently competitive, and they view every situation as a competition that they must win. This mindset can lead to a relentless pursuit of victory at all costs and can erode trust in you as a leader.

Guru Guidance

In many organizations, there is a strong emphasis on performance and results, often with little tolerance for failure. Consequently, leaders in such environments often feel compelled to "win" every interaction that they have during a workday. Resist this temptation. Business is a team sport where colleagues work together to achieve goals. For this reason, make compromise a part of your leadership repertoire.

Many people have a self-image that makes them believe that they must appear invincible. They see "winning" as the only way to validate their competence and leadership abilities. Anything less is perceived as a threat to their ego and pride.

Of course, most highly competitive people harbor a deep-rooted fear of failure, too. It is a common underpinning of the "must-win" mentality. Besides alienating their peers, leaders prone to this mindset worry that any loss or setback may result in criticism, job insecurity, or damage to their reputation.

> *"Leaders prone to this mindset worry that any loss or setback may result in criticism, job insecurity, or damage to their reputation ... "*

As a result, these leaders put their organizations at risk because they tend to be "lone wolves," who prioritize short-term gains and immediate victories over long-term sustainability and growth – regardless of the potential negative consequences that such an approach has on them or their organizations.

Clearly, you don't want to be this kind of leader!

DOI: 10.4324/9781003422754-91

Effective leadership requires a balanced style that acknowledges the importance of adapting to different situations, cooperating with peers, and learning from mistakes. Leaders who recognize the value of not having to "win" all the time create a more team-oriented workplace.

How to Put It into Action

For Executive-Level Leaders – Create an environment where team members feel obliged to discuss challenges, seek feedback, and propose solutions that require teamwork to accomplish.

For Mid-Level Leaders – Remove your ego from the work at hand. Instead, encourage yourself and your team of leaders to see every situation as an opportunity to work together as a team.

For Supervisory-Level Leaders – Stress the importance of collaboration and teamwork. Encourage your staffers to work together to solve problems and share credit for achievements, promoting the notion that business is a "*team sport.*"

Idea Crosswalk

- **Leadership Mindset** – A leader who is willing to cooperate fosters a collaborative and "team first" workplace.
- **Vision** – A vision that features the value of teamwork promotes trust and a sense of belonging among employees.
- **Company Culture** – A leader's willingness to keep their competitiveness in check sets the tone for a culture that values cooperation, open communication, and trust.
- **People and Talent** – Supportive leaders who empower their staffers tend to attract and retain talent who value teamwork and collaboration.
- **Change Management** – A leader who values cooperation is more likely to adopt change frameworks that involve employees in the decision-making process and leverage their expertise – reducing resistance to change.

Part VI

Change Management Tips

Indispensable leaders embrace change. Change is the one constant in any business. The best leaders recognize this fact and work to prepare their people to handle it with ease and a thirst to learn from the experience.

They know that perfection is elusive. So, an indispensable leader does not get consumed by the pursuit. Instead, they shift their thinking to the optimization of execution, which can enable the achievement of the best results in any situation.

Leaders adjust their style to enable change to occur. Just like a hammer is not always the best tool for every home improvement project, there is no "one" way to manage the changes needed within a business. As a consequence, the best leaders know how to adjust their styles to improve outcomes.

These tips help leaders to drive change within their organizations.

DOI: 10.4324/9781003422754-92

If not now, then when? If not you, then who?

A change-oriented leadership mindset inspires a sense of ownership and a commitment to drive needed changes, regardless of how challenging these changes may be to achieve.

Guru Guidance

Leaders must take responsibility for their actions and decisions. By asking, "If not me, then who?" leaders emphasize the idea that they are accountable for making things happen. Embrace it and see how things begin to happen for you and your organization!

A leader's change-oriented mindset drives proactive, accountable, and success-driven behavior throughout an organization.

Sure, there are many pressing challenges and opportunities that every leader must confront each day. Procrastination leads to missed chances and the acceleration of problems.

> *" . . . change-oriented leaders don't procrastinate."*

However, change-oriented leaders don't procrastinate. They recognize it is up to them to make changes for the good of the organization. They act decisively, drive progress and achieve goals.

Additionally, the most talented leaders recognize that taking calculated risks is part of the job of leading others. These kinds of leaders acknowledge the need to step out of their comfort zones to pursue opportunities. They choose to address challenges, head-on and without hesitation.

This mindset goes hand-in-hand with the notion that your time to lead is now. In fact, accepting the idea that "If not now, then when?" is an essential leadership tenet because it helps to proliferate urgency, responsibility, and accountability through the enterprise.

Together, these thoughts reinforce the significance of driving the changes that must be made to enable an organization to flourish.

DOI: 10.4324/9781003422754-93

How to Put It into Action

For Executive-Level Leaders – Ensure that your actions and decisions align with the organization's values, vision, and mission. This reinforces the importance of the "if not me, then whom" mindset in achieving the organization's objectives.

For Mid-Level Leaders – Create some urgency! Exceptional leaders create a sense of urgency by communicating the importance of taking action promptly. They emphasize the consequences of inaction and highlight the benefits of timely execution. So, take action and make it urgent!

For Supervisory-Level Leaders – Establish mechanisms for regular feedback and hold team members accountable for their actions. This reinforces the idea that actions have consequences and that everyone is responsible for their part.

Idea Crosswalk

- **Leadership Mindset** – This leadership ethos emphasizes accountability, taking initiative, and accepting responsibility for delivering results.
- **Vision** – A well-defined vision should inspire and motivate individuals to take responsibility for their part in achieving it.
- **Company Culture** – A culture that values individual initiative encourages employees to take ownership of their roles and responsibilities to contribute to the organization's success.
- **People and Talent** – Talent management systems should identify and nurture leadership potential, preparing change-oriented individuals to take on leadership roles as needed.
- **Trust and Empowerment** – A high level of trust creates an environment where leaders can be proactive in setting direction and inspiring others to change.

Know what you can control and make that better

Concentrating on controllable factors helps us maintain focus and avoid distractions.

Guru Guidance

When leaders understand what they control and focus on that, they are better positioned to tackle challenges and solve problems. This insight empowers them to address issues head-on and implement effective solutions within their realm of influence.

Essentially, understanding and improving what can be controlled helps leaders to operate more strategically, maintain focus, and drive positive change within their organizations.

> *" . . . recognizing what can be controlled allows leaders to make better strategic choices."*

After all, we only have so much time, energy, and resources. By concentrating on what we can control, our focus is allocated to actions we can use to maximize our impact on key areas that contribute to organizational success.

Yes, recognizing what can be controlled allows leaders to make better strategic choices.

Instead of squandering energy on issues beyond their control, they can invest time and attention in areas where they can have a meaningful impact and contribute to the achievement of strategic objectives.

To be sure, leaders who understand and accept the limits of control are better prepared to navigate change, too. This makes it easier for them to measure progress, evaluate performance, and make data-driven decisions that contribute to improved outcomes.

Also, communicating a clear understanding of what is controllable fosters confidence and trust among team members. Employees are more likely to be engaged and motivated when they see their leaders focus on factors that they can control to drive positive change.

DOI: 10.4324/9781003422754-94

How to Put It into Action

For Executive-Level Leaders – Empower team members by delegating responsibilities and decision-making authority. Trusting others with tasks that align with their expertise not only enhances a leader's ability to focus on strategic priorities but also fosters a sense of ownership among team members.

For Mid-Level Leaders – Conduct regular assessments of the internal environment and identify areas that are controllable and can be improved. Be sure to include processes, workflows, team dynamics, and other internal factors in your assessments.

For Supervisory-Level Leaders – Approach challenges with a problem-solving mindset. Leaders should encourage the team to identify solutions rather than dwelling on issues outside of their control. This promotes a more solution-oriented culture.

Idea Crosswalk

- **Leadership Mindset** – Knowing what you can control and striving to make those things better has a profound impact on various facets of a company.
- **Vision** – Leaders should shape their organization's vision to be realistic, achievable, and based on the organization's strengths and capabilities. Aspirational, yes; impossible, no!
- **Company Culture** – Leaders who understand their areas of influence can guide the organization through change more effectively, creating an agile culture that responds proactively to evolving circumstances.
- **People and Talent** – Employees are more likely to be engaged when they see leaders actively working on issues that are within their control to manage. This behavior drives a sense of purpose and confidence in staffers, too.
- **Trust and Empowerment** – Leaders who prioritize focusing on controllable factors are perceived as more effective, which encourages trust in their judgment.

You don't have to change the world for a change to be important

This realization leads to a pragmatic and impactful approach to leadership.

Guru Guidance

Embracing the idea that not every change has to be monumental fosters a growth mindset within the enterprise. Staffers are more likely to experiment, learn, and adapt when they know that leadership values progress, regardless of its scale.

Small changes involve less risk than large-scale initiatives. They allow businesses to test and iterate minimizing the potential for significant disruptions to the enterprise. This mitigates the risk of failure and provides the opportunity to fine-tune strategies based on real-world outcomes.

> *"For example, small changes in processes and workflows can lead to improved operational efficiencies . . ."*

For example, small changes in processes and workflows can lead to improved operational efficiencies, which often provide critical results for an organization, including cost reductions, time efficiencies, and stronger customer retention – supporting the idea that modest change can make a difference.

In fact, seemingly minor adjustments in customer interactions, service delivery, or product features can lead to a significantly improved customer experience and revenue growth. Enhancing the customer experience, even in small ways, will foster loyalty and a more positive brand value in the marketplace.

Certainly, in today's rapidly changing business landscape, staying ahead of competitors often involves making timely and targeted changes – even making the slightest adjustments based on customer feedback or industry trends can provide a competitive edge.

DOI: 10.4324/9781003422754-95

How to Put It into Action

For Executive-Level Leaders – Acknowledge and celebrate small victories within the organization. Even if the changes are modest, recognize the efforts of staffers who contribute to positive outcomes. It reinforces the idea that small wins matter and collectively can make a big difference.

For Mid-Level Leaders – Set realistic expectations for the pace of change. Recognize that your enterprise can achieve meaningful progress through a series of smaller, well-planned refinements on the way work is executed.

For Supervisory-Level Leaders – Embrace approaches that lead to organizational agility. Communicate that the ability to make swift, flexible adjustments in response to changing market conditions can be monumental, even when they're smaller in scope.

Idea Crosswalk

- **Leadership Mindset** – Leaders who possess a well-balanced change perspective often become more attuned to customer feedback and can make swift adjustments to products, services, or processes based on customer needs and preferences.
- **Vision** – The vision of the organization becomes more realistic and agile when its leaders espouse a practical approach to change.
- **Company Culture** – A culture that values impactful change, regardless of scope, is inherently a culture of continuous learning. This encourages employees to seek new knowledge and apply it for the good of the business.
- **People and Talent** – Implementing simple changes often involves the participation of various departments and teams, which enables staffers to learn from one another.
- **Trust and Empowerment** – Leaders who communicate openly about the importance of regular, incremental improvements build trust among employees, stakeholders, and customers. In turn, this leads to a more positive and trusted organizational reputation.

Leadership Tip 89

Use the "why" to inspire change

Knowing the reasons behind the change helps set realistic expectations. Employees can better understand what to expect during the transition and can mentally prepare for it.

Guru Guidance

When leaders don't provide a clear explanation of why a change is happening, rumors and misinformation spread. This can lead to confusion and anxiety among employees, which is detrimental to the change initiative. So, start your change work with the "why!"

> *"It is a fundamental step in change management that helps pave the way for a smoother transition."*

Indeed, explaining the "why" when embarking on change initiatives is essential for creating shared understanding, building trust, engaging employees, and ultimately, increasing the likelihood of success. It is a fundamental step in change management that helps pave the way for a smoother transition.

Further, it is the "why" that puts the change in context, helping employees see how it fits into the bigger picture. This helps staffers to connect the dots and understand how the proposed changes relate to their work.

Transparency is also enhanced by clarifying why a change is necessary. It builds trust with employees, too. When people believe that leaders are being open and honest about the reasons for change, they are more likely to trust the leader to lead the way.

In addition, a sense of purpose and motivation propagates among staffers when they better understand how a proposed change helps the enterprise achieve its vision. Indeed, the better staff members understand the reason for the change, the lower their resistance, and anxiety about it. This helps them to get behind and contribute to the success of the initiative.

DOI: 10.4324/9781003422754-96

How to Put It into Action

For Executive-Level Leaders – Use storytelling to illustrate the current challenges, the envisioned future, and the positive impact of the change. Stories can make the "*why*" more relatable.

For Mid-Level Leaders – Clearly articulate the benefits of the change, both for the organization and for your team of leaders. Be sure to answer the question: "What will improve, and how will it positively impact individuals and teams?"

For Supervisory-Level Leaders – Avoid sugarcoating the situation. Be honest about any difficulties or challenges the change may present and describe your confidence in making the change happen when providing your team with the "why."

Idea Crosswalk

- **Leadership Mindset** – Starting with "why" ensures that leaders and the entire leadership team are aligned on the fundamental purpose and goals for a given change effort.
- **Vision** – The "why" provides a clear and compelling vision for the organization. It helps leaders and employees understand where the organization is headed and why it's worth the effort.
- **Company Culture** – An organization that starts with "why" often has a higher level of accountability, both from leadership and among employees, "baked into" its culture.
- **People and Talent** – A compelling "why" improves employee retention as people are more likely to stay with a company that they believe in and see a future with.
- **Trust and Empowerment** – Trust is enhanced when employees understand the reason why a change is needed.

Change comes one person at a time

Each employee must be convinced that a given change is worth making. So, change strategies must be aimed at helping each person choose to change.

Guru Guidance

Find and engage your change agents! Business change starts with individuals who are willing to embrace, champion, and lead the change. These individuals serve as change ambassadors, influencing their peers and gradually building momentum for broader organizational transformation.

No one can change another. Each person needs to choose to change on their own. This can be accomplished through a variety of means. For example, the work becoming easier, more interesting, offering greater opportunity, and the threat of job loss (if changes aren't made) can often loom large in a person's decision to change. So, be sure to lay those issues out when asking people to change.

> *"As more individuals personally accept and adapt to the changes, the more they become ingrained in the organizational culture . . . "*

With that, leaders can speed up the process of staffers choosing to change by engaging influential employees to assist. Contemporaries can often sway the attitudes and behaviors of their peers. The practice tends to have a cascading effect, as well – inspiring others to choose to change, too.

Of course, despite your best efforts, people may still resist change. Sometimes it is due to fear of the unknown or other misconceptions. Individual attention and support can address their fears and help them to transition more smoothly.

As more individuals personally accept and adapt to changes, the more they become ingrained in the organizational culture, leading to the transformation of the entire enterprise.

DOI: 10.4324/9781003422754-97

How to Put It into Action

For Executive-Level Leaders – Encourage a culture of continuous improvement, where everyone is committed to personal and professional development.

For Mid-Level Leaders – Be patient and persistent with your team of leaders, recognizing that not everyone will adapt to change at the same pace.

For Supervisory-Level Leaders – Respect the autonomy of team members. People are more likely to embrace change when they feel they have a degree of control over their own adaptation process.

Idea Crosswalk

- **Leadership Mindset** – Leaders who prioritize individual well-being and professional development will be more inclined to support personalized change efforts.
- **Vision** – If the vision includes adaptability, innovation, or a commitment to continuous improvement, it will reinforce the importance of change acceptance at an individual level.
- **Company Culture** – A culture that values learning, experimentation, and adaptation will boost the willingness of staffers to change.
- **People and Talent** – Leaders must trust their team members to make meaningful changes, and team members must trust their leaders to support and guide them through the process.
- **Trust and Empowerment** – Empowerment is essential for change at the individual level. When team members feel empowered, they are more likely to seize opportunities to change and improve.

Quality is a habit

Consistently producing high-quality work is the result of ingrained habits and practices.

Guru Guidance

Quality isn't achieved through occasional effort; it's the result of consistently following best practices, paying attention to detail, and maintaining high standards. When these habits become entrenched within an enterprise, outcomes improve.

> *" . . . a detail orientation has to be 'designed' into an organization through its values and norms."*

Making quality a habit involves cultivating a mindset within the workforce that values attention to detail, precision, and excellence. Over time, this mindset becomes second nature, influencing every aspect of work.

But a detail orientation has to be "designed" into an organization through its values and norms. When done right, quality work becomes a habit.

Indeed, in organizations where quality has become a habit, there exists an unquenchable thirst for improvement. These enterprises make sure that quality never becomes a one-time thing by instituting reliable, repeatable processes that are followed by everyone within the concern.

By streamlining and standardizing business processes, staffers can fully understand exactly what needs to be done to maintain high standards. In turn, this helps employees to develop a mindset that is based on excellence.

Truly, when quality becomes a habit within an organization, it's never dependent on individual effort. Rather, it's just how work gets done there.

DOI: 10.4324/9781003422754-98

How to Put It into Action

For Executive-Level Leaders – Recognize that instituting quality as a habit is a long-term commitment. Be prepared to unswervingly reinforce the importance of quality in what you say and do.

For Mid-Level Leaders – Insufficient resources can hinder quality efforts. Ensure that employees have the necessary resources, support, and time required to consistently produce high-quality work.

For Supervisory-Level Leaders – Actively involve employees in discussions about quality improvement. Their perspectives and insights can be invaluable in identifying areas for workplace enhancement.

Idea Crosswalk

- **Leadership Mindset** – Leaders who emphasize and enable quality can set a company apart and make it a desirable place to work and do business with.
- **Vision** – A quality-centered vision can differentiate a company in the market, attract like-minded staffers, and inspire them to bring their best effort to work each day.
- **Company Culture** – Quality as a habit fosters a culture of excellence. Team members are encouraged to take pride in their work, hold themselves to high standards, and strive for continuous improvement.
- **People and Talent** – A focus on quality supports talent development by encouraging employees to continually learn, adapt, and grow in their roles.
- **Trust and Empowerment** – Quality-driven companies empower employees to identify and address issues on the spot, which builds trust and helps to make quality a habit within the workplace.

Awareness is the greatest change tool in your arsenal

It empowers us to understand ourselves, our teams, our business, and the need for change.

Guru Guidance

Leaders who possess a high degree of self-awareness better understand their strengths, weaknesses, and biases. This enables them to recognize when they need to improve in order to lead the changes required by their organizations.

Awareness of one's emotions, and the emotions of others, is crucial for effective leadership. Leaders who recognize and manage their emotions, and help team members manage their own, create a more poised and confident workforce.

> " . . . the best leaders are attuned to the needs, concerns, and perspectives of their staffers."

Indeed, the best leaders are attuned to the needs, concerns, and perspectives of their staffers. This enables them to build strong relationships, foster collaboration, and motivate their employees.

Further, when leaders have greater situational awareness, they are more effective communicators who are able to match the message to the audience. This awareness helps reduce resistance and increase buy-in from employees. This contributes to making change initiatives more successful.

Likewise, better awareness helps leaders make better decisions. Strategic options are better understood when leaders possess a clear understanding of their organization's strengths and weaknesses, market conditions, and emerging opportunities. In turn, this leads to the "right" choices being more readily.

DOI: 10.4324/9781003422754-99

How to Put It into Action

For Executive-Level Leaders – Cultivate empathy to better understand the feelings and experiences of your team members. This can help build trust and rapport, as well as improve your ability to determine the changes needed to propel the business forward.

For Mid-Level Leaders – Accept that change is inevitable, and be prepared to adapt your tactics and decisions as circumstances evolve. An awareness of shifting dynamics and a willingness to adjust to them is valuable leadership traits to cultivate.

For Supervisory-Level Leaders – Actively seek feedback from peers, subordinates, and superiors. Constructive feedback derived from various parts of the enterprise can provide valuable insights into what changes are needed to improve the business.

Idea Crosswalk

- **Leadership Mindset** – Increased self-awareness can lead to more authentic leadership. When leaders are aware of their strengths and weaknesses, they are more likely to lead with honesty and transparency. Authentic leadership builds trust and credibility with employees.
- **Vision** – Awareness of market trends and changes in the external environment allows leaders to adapt their vision and strategies more quickly, which enables firms to seize new opportunities.
- **Company Culture** – Leaders with high awareness tend to be more attuned to employee well-being. They prioritize work-life integration, mental health, and stress management, leading to a healthier and more supportive change culture.
- **People and Talent** – Leaders who are aware of their team members' needs and aspirations can better engage and motivate their people during change efforts – working to tie the work at hand to their staffer's wants and desires.
- **Trust and Empowerment** – Greater awareness creates a more supportive and trustful work environment that is better equipped to adapt to change, meet challenges, and achieve long-term success.

Technology is a tool, not a solution

Throwing technology at a problem won't necessarily solve it. In fact, sometimes it makes it worse.

Guru Guidance

Technology can be a powerful and valuable enabler, but it should not be seen as a panacea that solves all problems on its own. Rather, you need to get the people and process design right first, then apply technology to assist people in doing the work at hand.

Too many leaders believe that technology is all that is needed to make the business better. But technology is really just another tool that can be part of a solution – it is not a solution in and of itself. The fact is technology needs to be thoughtfully integrated into a broader strategy and applied where it can be leveraged in support of realizing the organization's vision.

> " . . . *the effectiveness of technology depends on the specific context in which it is applied.*"

Further, the effectiveness of technology depends on the specific context in which it is applied. What works as a solution in one situation may not work in another. The appropriateness of a particular technology depends on the problem it is meant to address and the related operational environment where it will be put to use.

Also, technology evolves and becomes obsolete. What is considered state-of-the-art technology today may become outdated in a few years. Therefore, technology solutions need to be adaptable and flexible to remain effective. Relying on technology without a plan for long-term evolution and support can lead to problems down the road.

To sum up, strategy-setting is where solutions to business problems are discovered. It requires human judgment, creativity, and emotional intelligence. Even the most sophisticated technology cannot replicate those

DOI: 10.4324/9781003422754-100

characteristics. Complex decision-making, empathy, and innovative thinking are essential components of determining strategies where technology can be leveraged as tools in support of the enterprise.

How to Put It into Action

For Executive-Level Leaders – Ensure that your organization's use of technology is aligned with the overall strategic goals of the enterprise. Technology should be viewed as a means to achieve these objectives, not an end in itself.

For Mid-Level Leaders – Establish the connection between strategy and the use of technology as an enabler in your team of leader's minds. This will help them to find uses of technology in support of the organization's mission.

For Supervisory-Level Leaders – Encourage and support digital literacy and skill development within the organization. Ensure that your team members have the necessary knowledge and skills to effectively use technology as a tool to complete their work.

Idea Crosswalk

- **Leadership Mindset** – Leaders who have a vision for how technology can enhance their organization's operations and achieve its goals are more likely to embrace and drive technology adoption.
- **Vision** – A well-defined vision for the organization should include the strategic use of technology as a means to achieve its goals.
- **Company Culture** – Leaders play a pivotal role in fostering a culture that encourages experimentation, learning from failures, and the creative use of technology.
- **People and Talent** – Effective people management involves identifying skill gaps and providing opportunities for staffers to acquire the digital skills needed to use technology as a tool.
- **Trust and Empowerment** – Technology can make the workplace more productive and serve as a great "equalizer" that enhances trust among workers of all capabilities.

Design work as if it's done by one!

Staffers become more satisfied with their work when it is designed to be efficient and free from unnecessary obstacles.

Guru Guidance

Ultimately, customer satisfaction is the best measure of process improvement. When customers receive what they need, when they need it, they are more likely to be loyal and advocate for the business. So, it's why to streamline with the customer in mind.

It's strategic to improve efficiency, reduce waste, and enhance customer satisfaction in the spirit of achieving a competitive edge in the marketplace. While not the intent, designing work so it could conceivably be done by one person enables leaders to better see the kinds of process changes and technology applications that could be put in place to optimize the way work is done.

> *" . . . employees have more time and mental space for innovation and creativity when they don't have to deal with constant operational disruptions . . . "*

Further, optimized workflow designs encourage collaboration between different parts of the organization. Cross-functional teams work together more effectively when they can rely on a smooth exchange of work throughout the enterprise's value chain.

Add to this the fact that employees have more time and mental space for innovation and creativity when they don't have to deal with constant operational disruptions, and you can come to appreciate the wisdom of continuously improving and optimizing workflow.

There's no question that, in today's fast-paced business environment, organizations must be agile and responsive to customer needs. Seamless workflows enable quicker response times and lead to improved customer satisfaction.

DOI: 10.4324/9781003422754-101

How to Put It into Action

For Executive-Level Leaders – Clearly define the objectives and outcomes that the organization seeks to achieve by improving workflow design. This might include reducing lead times, increasing productivity, or enhancing quality, for example.

For Mid-Level Leaders – Involve your team of leaders in workflow redesign. Because they're closer to the action, they usually have valuable insights and suggestions for streamlining the ways in which work can be done within their areas of responsibility.

For Supervisory-Level Leaders – Standardize processes where possible to create consistency and predictability.

Idea Crosswalk

- **Leadership Mindset** – A leader's emphasis on workflow optimization helps to instill execution excellence as an organizational value.
- **Vision** – Most strategic visions allude to flawless execution as a means of making the business the best it can be.
- **Company Culture** – Breaking down silos and redesigning workflows for efficiency makes the culture more collaborative and unified.
- **People and Talent** – Employee engagement gets a lift when staff sees that their leaders are committed to making their work more efficient.
- **Trust and Empowerment** – Workflow optimization often includes setting clear expectations and accountability mechanisms. Commitments are taken more seriously when leaders hold themselves and others accountable – fostering a culture of trust.

Always align decision rights with responsibilities

It allows leaders to leverage the collective expertise that exists within the enterprise and distribute decision-making authority lower into the organization where it's most effective.

Guru Guidance

Proper decision rights alignment enables staffers to operate better within their areas of responsibility. They can make real-time adjustments and redistribute effort as needed to address changing circumstances or unexpected challenges without needing to escalate for approval.

Aligning decision rights with job responsibilities is a central aspect of effective organizational management. It enhances accountability, efficiency, employee empowerment, and innovation, while also contributing to improved employee and customer satisfaction.

> *"Decentralized decision-making brings faster problem resolution . . . "*

Indeed, properly aligned decision rights help to streamline decision-making within the enterprise. Decentralized decision-making brings faster problem resolution – often enhancing the customer experience.

Additionally, it enables staff members to take ownership of their work. They have the autonomy to make decisions within their domains of expertise, which leads to increased enthusiasm and job satisfaction.

Likewise, senior leaders create more time for themselves to focus on more strategic tasks by delegating decision-making power down to properly prepared staffers at lower levels of the organization.

How to Put It into Action

For Executive-Level Leaders – See to it that decision rights are periodically reviewed within the organization. Assess whether current decision

DOI: 10.4324/9781003422754-102

rights are effective, and make adjustments as the organization evolves or as new challenges arise.

For Mid-Level Leaders – Address conflicts over decision authority promptly and transparently among your team of leaders. Seek to resolve disagreements through open communication and negotiation.

For Supervisory-Level Leaders – Create decision-making frameworks or guidelines that outline which decisions can be made at different levels of your team. Be sure that these are weaved into job descriptions and performance review criteria.

Idea Crosswalk

- **Leadership Mindset** – Leaders must be committed to moving decision-making authority down to the lowest suitable level of the enterprise to better empower their staffers.
- **Vision** – A vision that pushes decision authority lower into the organization makes for a more agile and adaptable enterprise.
- **Company Culture** – Decision rights optimization contributes to a culture of autonomy and accountability.
- **People and Talent** – Most people are drawn to organizations that empower their staff. Getting its decision rights correct can make an organization more attractive to prospective talent.
- **Trust and Empowerment** – When employees have decision rights, they are more likely to take their responsibilities seriously. This reinforces a culture of accountability and helps trust to grow within the organization.

Measure and reward desired behaviors

When specific behaviors are linked to performance metrics, employees are motivated to change behavior and improve their performance.

Guru Guidance

Measuring and rewarding desired behaviors promotes consistency in the workplace. When employees see that certain behaviors are consistently recognized and rewarded, they are more likely to adopt those behaviors as norms.

Measuring and rewarding desired behaviors is a powerful management technique that helps shape organizational culture, motivate employees, and drive performance in alignment with the organization's vision. It reinforces positive behaviors and supports the achievement of strategic objectives.

> *"It reinforces positive behaviors and supports the achievement of strategic objectives."*

When leaders do a good job of aligning measurements and rewards, they establish clear expectations for their employees. This clarity enables staffers to understand what is valued and what they are expected to achieve in their roles.

Further, recognizing and rewarding employees for exhibiting desired behaviors boosts their motivation and engagement. It provides positive reinforcement and encourages individuals to continue practicing those behaviors while setting the bar for others to clear so they can gain the same recognition and rewards.

In fact, when conflicts or misunderstandings arise over staffer performance, proper measurement criteria can provide a reference point for resolving disputes. When done right, the measurement and reward framework indicates what is considered appropriate and valued behavior within an enterprise.

DOI: 10.4324/9781003422754-103

How to Put It into Action

For Executive-Level Leaders – Ensure that the organization is being transparent about its measurement criteria and reward system. Employees should understand how their performance is being assessed and how rewards are determined.

For Mid-Level Leaders – Safeguard that the measurement and reward system is consistently applied and that all staffers have equal opportunities to be recognized and rewarded for demonstrating the desired behaviors.

For Supervisory-Level Leaders – Tailor the measurement and reward system to accommodate different roles and responsibilities within your team, recognizing that not all positions will exhibit the same behaviors, so they must be customized based on job requirements.

Idea Crosswalk

- **Leadership Mindset** – Leaders should reward behaviors and actions that lead to better organizational outcomes.
- **Vision** – A measurement and reward system that reinforces the behaviors required to succeed in the marketplace is essential to vision achievement.
- **Company Culture** – Measuring and rewarding desired behaviors reinforces the organization's culture.
- **People and Talent** – People strategies must align with the measurement and reward system to equip employees with the skills and competencies needed to improve their adoption of desired behaviors.
- **Trust and Empowerment** – A transparent and fair measurement and reward system builds trust among employees.

"Go WEST" to make change more palatable

WEST is an acronym worth remembering.

Guru Guidance

I've used this approach with great success countless times. It has worked for me. I know that it will work for you, too!

An easy way to address people's resistance to change is to "go WEST." It's an acronym for a change technique that I developed in my consulting practice. Here's what it means:

> *"Give your team the time it needs to make change happen for the organization."*

- **Why**: As in, provide the "why." Help people understand what's in it for them. Show them that the proposed change can improve the work situation for your team.
- **Evangelists**: Engage people who can evangelize and support the change within the organization. Enthusiasm is contagious. Others will buy in when supporters endorse the changes that you want to make.
- **Smaller Parts**: Break a major change initiative into smaller, more "digestible" pieces that can be accomplished readily by the organization. Early and regular successes will establish the needed momentum to keep a change effort moving smartly forward.
- **Time**: Change requires time. So, be patient. Give your team the time it needs to make change happen for the organization. You will be pleasantly surprised to discover how much can be accomplished, if you keep your impatience in check.

Give my "go WEST" approach a try on your next major change initiative and see the difference it can make for you.

DOI: 10.4324/9781003422754-104

How to Put It into Action

For Executive-Level Leaders – When kicking off your next change effort, highlight the benefits and advantages that the change will bring, both to the organization and to individuals. People are more likely to get behind and support a change project when they see how it can improve their lives. It is an important part of sharing the "why."

For Mid-Level Leaders – When briefing your team on a new change effort, be sure to share previous success stories that demonstrate the positive impact that similar initiatives have delivered in the past. It will help you recruit *evangelists* to the cause.

For Supervisory-Level Leaders – Give your people the time needed to make change happen. Your patience will pay dividends in the long run.

Idea Crosswalk

- **Leadership Mindset** – Leaders who exhibit patience demonstrate a steadfast commitment to the change initiative.
- **Vision** – Incremental change can become an important theme of your vision story. It suggests the value of breaking bigger change efforts into smaller, more manageable parts.
- **Company Culture** – Change evangelists can drive cultural change by modeling the desired behaviors and values associated with the change initiative. They can help create a culture that is more receptive to change and innovation.
- **People and Talent** – Leaders who provide the "why" of a change initiative reduce stress and anxiety among staffers during times of change.
- **Trust and Empowerment** – Leaders who are authentic and genuine, reinforce the trust needed to "go WEST."

Sometimes you need to go slow to go fast!

An oxymoron, perhaps, though truer words have never been written.

Guru Guidance

Prioritizing quality over speed often yields better long-term results. A rushed approach may lead to errors and rework, which can be time-consuming and costly to fix. Going slow and getting things right the first time can prevent more expensive "fixes" down the road.

After all, good things take time. Rushing to get things done introduces needless risk, leads to error, and, generally, creates drama where there ordinarily would be none.

Slow and deliberate planning and execution, on the other hand, can help identify and mitigate risks, preventing potential setbacks that could slow down progress. Good upfront work results in smoother and faster execution.

> *"Rushing to get things done introduces needless risk . . . "*

Furthermore, going slow in building a strong organizational foundation, including infrastructure, processes, and culture, can create a more stable and resilient enterprise – one that is better equipped to handle setbacks and rapid growth with similar aplomb.

Indeed, the principle of "going slow to go fast" emphasizes the importance of taking a measured and deliberate approach to business operations, planning, and decision-making – and, by taking the time to get it right, leaders can avoid costly mistakes, adapt more effectively, and position themselves for greater success over the long-term.

Remember, going slow allows for learning and adaptation. When organizations take the time to gather data, analyze trends, and learn from past experiences, they can make better-informed decisions and adapt quickly when necessary.

DOI: 10.4324/9781003422754-105

How to Put It into Action

For Executive-Level Leaders – Focus on building a strong organizational foundation, which includes effective processes, robust infrastructure, and a positive workplace. A well-structured organization can respond to opportunities and challenges more swiftly.

For Mid-Level Leaders – Slow down! When implementing organizational changes, take the time to engage employees, provide clear communication, and address concerns. In the long run, a well-managed change process leads to less disruption and faster implementation.

For Supervisory-Level Leaders – Provide opportunities for skill development and invest in the resources necessary for efficient execution. Well-prepared teams work more effectively and consistently deliver on expectations.

Idea Crosswalk

- **Leadership Mindset** – Leaders who embrace this philosophy develop a strategic mindset – one that appreciates the value of longer-term impact over shorter-term gains.
- **Vision** – The "go slow to go fast" mindset enables an organization's long-term strategic success by reminding staffers that getting it right now is less expensive than fixing it later.
- **Company Culture** – Higher performing company cultures are ones where employees appreciate that they are responsible for delivering quality results and taking shortcuts is not a path to success.
- **People and Talent** – Employees feel better about their work when they have realistic and attainable goals, ones that they don't feel rushed to accomplish.
- **Trust and Empowerment** – Embracing the philosophy builds trust in leadership's decision-making abilities. It shows that leaders are willing to make tough decisions and prioritize quality over haste.

Create learning moments to make your people stronger

Learning moments provide the space for reflection. Teams can assess their progress, identify what's working and what's not, and make informed adjustments.

Guru Guidance

Moments of collaborative learning enhance team cohesion. When team members learn together, it fosters a sense of camaraderie and shared purpose. This boosts morale and makes a team more resilient in the face of challenges.

> *"Solid knowledge sharing leads to improved ways of thinking and doing . . . "*

Organizations strengthen their people and enhance their ability to successfully navigate the complexities of change by making learning an integral part of the change process.

Let's face it; change initiatives often involve complex problems. Learning moments allow team members to break down these problems, analyze them, and generate creative solutions. Problem-solving capacity is expanded as people derive lessons while performing change management activities.

Further, staffers working on change initiatives need to be adaptable, as the external environment and circumstances often shift unexpectedly. Emphasizing what is to be learned when conditions change helps team members become more flexible and better equipped to manage and respond to unexpected situations.

Also, creating opportunities to learn encourages the sharing of insights and best practices among team members. Solid knowledge sharing leads to improved ways of thinking and doing throughout the enterprise as others learn from those who have encountered similar situations in the past.

Indeed, when team members are actively involved in learning and problem-solving, they take greater ownership of the change initiative.

DOI: 10.4324/9781003422754-106

Their engagement in the effort increases as progress is made. Leaders should look for opportunities to help teams learn from the work that they're doing.

How to Put It into Action

For Executive-Level Leaders – After encountering obstacles or setbacks, hold debrief sessions to analyze what happened, why it happened, and how to prevent similar issues in the future. This exercise can lead to valuable insights and lessons for the executive team.

For Mid-Level Leaders – Encourage team members to derive innovative solutions and ideas related to the change initiative. Support their experimentation and provide a "safe space" for learning to occur.

For Supervisory-Level Leaders – Dedicate time in team meetings for reflection. Ask staffers to share what they've learned recently and how they plan to apply that knowledge moving forward.

Idea Crosswalk

- **Leadership Mindset** – Leaders who emphasize "learning by doing" demonstrate a commitment to personal and organizational growth.
- **Vision** – A culture of learning fosters innovative thinking. Innovation is a vision story imperative.
- **Company Culture** – A culture that values the sharing of "lessons learned" increases information sharing, collaboration, and teamwork.
- **People and Talent** – Cultivating learning moments can boost employee engagement. Team members who feel that their growth and development are supported tend to be more motivated and committed to change efforts.
- **Trust and Empowerment** – The spirit of "learning as you go" increases trust in the change process itself. Team members better understand the value of learning from experience and adjusting as needed.

It's OK to shut it down!

Continuously pushing forward with a change initiative that is not delivering can damage morale. Staffers often lose confidence in their leaders's ability to make wise decisions and manage change effectively.

Guru Guidance

When resources are tied up in an underperforming initiative, it can prevent the organization from pursuing other potentially more successful opportunities. Shutting down a failing initiative frees up resources that can be reapplied to more promising endeavors.

> "Unfortunately, some change efforts don't seem to ever have an end."

Change efforts are a journey. They have a definite beginning and middle. Unfortunately, some change efforts don't seem to ever have an end. Most runaway projects appear to be too big to change. We feel trapped by their scope. We can't seem to close them out short of achieving the goal. So, we extend the scope, or worse, start all over again.

To combat falling victim to a never-ending change initiative, remember you have the opportunity (dare I say, responsibility) to call it a game when the effort has no clear end in sight. Indeed, you can close down a current initiative and move on to something more promising.

Also, adopting a mindset that recognizes that major change efforts should be organized into a series of smaller, more finite pieces that can be better managed lowers risk. In fact, it enables easier disengagement from change initiatives that are not panning out, while providing opportunities to double down on those that are delivering better-than-expected outcomes.

Of course, the decision to shut down a change initiative should be made thoughtfully and based on a thorough assessment of the reasons for underperformance. Sometimes, adjustments, restructuring, or a phased

DOI: 10.4324/9781003422754-107

approach may be more appropriate than outright termination. Regardless, it is a leader's responsibility to make the call on the best way to proceed.

How to Put It into Action

For Executive-Level Leaders – Use your sponsorship authority to ensure that change initiatives being done under your watch are delivering as planned. When they're not, and the remediation efforts are falling short, pull the plug.

For Mid-Level Leaders – Keep your sponsors apprised of project status and give your best advice regarding the long-term prospects of success. Recommend that a never-ending project be shut down if it is not delivering as planned.

For Supervisory-Level Leaders – Don't report status as "*green*," if your project is running in the "*red*." Provide honest status reporting so your management team can take corrective action or close out a runaway project.

Idea Crosswalk

- **Leadership Mindset** – Leaders should recognize the practice of closing down a runaway project as a sign of enhanced risk awareness and improved decisiveness.
- **Vision** – Transparency and open communication are critical elements of most vision stories. Leaders who communicate the reasons for the decision to shut down a poor-performing project reinforce their commitment to the vision.
- **Company Culture** – Leaders should encourage employees to view project failures as opportunities for growth and learning, promoting a more hardy workplace culture.
- **People and Talent** – The experience of closing down a runaway project often helps to prevent employee burnout and frustration, while serving to enhance staffer morale.
- **Trust and Empowerment** – While shutting down a current project can initially erode trust among employees, how leaders handle the aftermath is crucial. If they take responsibility and seek to learn from the experience, the organization's trust quotient is strengthened.

Don't take it too seriously – things will change

Leaders who are too set in their ways may struggle to adapt to change, potentially hindering the growth and success of their organizations.

Guru Guidance

Leaders who take things too seriously may stifle creativity and discourage risk-taking, both of which are crucial for fostering innovation within an enterprise. So, take a deep breath and ease up. Recognize that situations will change and it's up to you to lead the way!

A stern and inflexible leadership style will negatively impact employee morale and engagement. However, when leaders are approachable and open to new ideas, staffers feel more empowered to contribute their thoughts and suggestions, creating a more positive and collaborative work environment.

> *"A stern and inflexible leadership style will negatively impact employee morale . . ."*

Clearly, setbacks and failures are inevitable. Leaders who take themselves, or their work, too seriously may find it challenging to bounce back from setbacks. On the other hand, leaders who recognize that things change with time tend to maintain a healthier perspective and possess greater resilience during tough times.

In fact, leaders who balance seriousness with a sense of humor often find it easier to communicate with their teams. Their lighthearted approach gives their people confidence that all is not lost, even when things aren't going as planned.

Of course, business leaders need to take their responsibilities seriously, but they also need to maintain a flexible and relaxed mindset to navigate the ever-changing business landscape successfully. A healthy dose of humor, humility, and a willingness to embrace change is good not only for leaders but for their people, too.

DOI: 10.4324/9781003422754-108

How to Put It into Action

For Executive-Level Leaders – Show your willingness to embrace change with a positive attitude and encourage a culture where adaptation is valued. This can involve adjusting strategies, enhancing business processes, or even adjusting the organizational structure when necessary.

For Mid-Level Leaders – Maintain an optimistic outlook when admitting to mistakes and taking responsibility when things go sideways. Leaders who can smile when confronting missteps foster a culture that learns and grows.

For Supervisory-Level Leaders – Inject some humor into the workplace. It can help create a positive atmosphere. Leaders who can laugh at themselves and share light moments foster a more relaxed and enjoyable work environment.

Idea Crosswalk

- **Leadership Mindset** – A balanced and adaptable attitude sets a precedent for open communication, flexibility, and a willingness to evolve, creating a culture where leaders are seen as guides and coaches rather than uncompromising authorities.
- **Vision** – Leaders who embrace change with a positive mindset are more likely to foster innovation and keep the company's vision aligned with evolving market trends, technological advancements, and customer needs.
- **Company Culture** – A healthy blend of seriousness and flexibility promotes a workplace where employees feel valued, engaged, and encouraged to contribute their best.
- **People and Talent** – Individuals seek workplaces that offer opportunities for growth, and leaders who can take things in stride.
- **Trust and Empowerment** – Demonstrating a balanced attitude builds trust between leaders and their teams.

Closing Thoughts

I trust that you have discovered these 101 Leadership Tips to be a valuable resource, offering insights and strategies to enhance your ability to inspire, develop, and lead others.

But, we are not done, yet!

The aim is for this collection of ideas to play a significant role in your leadership evolution going forward, empowering you to effectively chart the course for your organization and navigate personal change as you strive for leadership excellence.

Make it a daily companion, and I am confident that you will begin to see yourself becoming an indispensable leader.

Above all else, remember that leadership is a choice!

DOI: 10.4324/9781003422754-109

The Last Word

I hope that you liked the book and the 101 indispensable leadership tips presented here.

For additional leadership content and information on my other management consulting services and offerings, please be sure to check out:

https://indispensable-consulting.com/

Also, I offer Executive, Middle Management and Supervisory-level Leadership Coaching programs, which enables you to provide personalized coaching for your entire leadership team and your most promising aspiring leaders.

Both programs use a combination of personal assessment and peer input to create the "right" coaching plan for each participant. We use the plan to drive the weekly 1-on-1 coaching sessions that I have with each person during the program. For more on these offerings, please see:

https://indispensable-coaching.com/

Lastly, if you're interested in booking me to speak at your next company event or conference, please contact me at:

jim@indispensable-consulting.com

I speak on topics related to leadership, company culture, vision storytelling, and the future of work. It is a terrific way for you to bring some extra value-added leadership ideas and insights to your colleagues.

Thank you!

DOI: 10.4324/9781003422754-110

Index